# Spear of the Nation

## (Umkhonto weSizwe)

T0170816

# OHIO SHORT HISTORIES OF AFRICA

This series of Ohio Short Histories of Africa is meant for those who are looking for a brief but lively introduction to a wide range of topics of South African history, politics, and biography, written by some of the leading experts in their fields.

# Spear of the Nation

# (Umkhonto weSizwe)

## SOUTH AFRICA'S LIBERATION ARMY,
1960s–1990s

Janet Cherry

OHIO UNIVERSITY PRESS
ATHENS

Ohio University Press, Athens, Ohio 45701
www.ohioswallow.com
All rights reserved

First published by Jacana Media (Pty) Ltd in 2011
Second impression 2011

10 Orange Street
Sunnyside
Auckland Park 2092
South Africa
(+27 11) 628-3200
www.jacana.co.za

© Janet Cherry, 2011

To obtain permission to quote, reprint, or otherwise reproduce
or distribute material from Ohio University Press publications,
please contact our rights and permissions department at (740)
593-1154 or (740) 593-4536 (fax).

First published in North America in 2012 by Ohio University Press
Printed in the United States of America
Ohio University Press books are printed on acid-free paper ♾ ™

20 19 18 17 16 15 14 13 12     5 4 3 2 1

ISBN: 978-0-8214-2026-3
e-ISBN: 978-0-8214-4443-6

*Library of Congress Cataloging-in-Publication Data available upon
request.*

Cover design by Joey Hi-Fi

# Contents

# Preface

I should like to thank Howard Barrell, Mzolisi Dyasi, Kholi Mhlana, Madeleine Fullard and Ronnie Kasrils for their comments on the manuscript, as well as the South African Democracy Education Trust (SADET) and the Port Elizabeth *amabutho* for their contributions. The opinions expressed here are my own.

1

# Introduction

Hailed as heroes by many South Africans, demonised as evil terrorists by others, Umkhonto weSizwe, the Spear of the Nation, is now part of history. Though the organisation no longer exists, its former members are represented by the MK Military Veterans' Association, which still carries some political clout within the ruling African National Congress (ANC).

The story of MK, as Umkhonto is widely and colloquially known in South Africa, is one of paradox and contradiction, successes and failures. A people's army fighting a people's war of national liberation, they never got to march triumphant into Pretoria. A small group of dedicated revolutionaries trained by the Soviet Union and its allies, they were committed to the seizure of state power, but instead found their principals engaged in negotiated settlement with the enemy as the winds of global politics shifted in the late 1980s. A guerrilla army of a few thousand soldiers in exile, disciplined and well trained, many of them were never deployed in battle, and most could not 'get home' to engage the enemy. Though MK soldiers set off limpet mines in public places in South Africa, killing a number of innocent civilians, they refrained from laying the anti-personnel mines that killed and maimed hundreds of thousands in other late-twentieth-century wars. They acted with remarkable restraint, and in doing so prevented a bloody race war from engulfing South Africa in the 1980s; yet they were accused of fostering a climate of insurrectionary violence in which nearly a thousand people were 'necklaced', and thousands more were shot, stabbed or hacked to death in violence involving civilians.

MK was arguably the last of the great liberation armies of the twentieth century – the freedom fighters who fought for independence from colonial, authoritarian or imperialist rule, in Vietnam and Bolivia, Guinea-Bissau and Nicaragua. In terms of international humanitarian law, the armed struggle that MK fought was a just war. At the same time, it was also one of the final conflicts of the Cold War era. MK's ideology, strategy and tactics acquired shape and took purchase within the great contest of the second half of the twentieth century between capitalism and socialism, between the West and the Communist bloc. The collapse of the Soviet Union and the end of the Cold War coincided with, and was a causal factor in, the end of MK's armed struggle and the negotiated transition to democracy in South Africa.

This book provides a brief history of MK, of which there are conflicting views and analyses. It does not present a detailed chronological account of every MK action but outlines the different strategic phases in its 30-odd-year history. It also illustrates these phases with stories drawn from the experiences of MK members. Some are taken from interviews conducted for the South African Democracy Education Trust project. I am indebted to SADET, who is the copyright-holder, for the opportunity to conduct some of these interviews and for access to others. Other stories are drawn from testimony to the Truth and Reconciliation Commission, whose records are in the public domain. There is some bias in the selection of illustrative material, mainly geographic in nature: I have been living in the Eastern Cape for over 25 years, and many of the stories and accounts come from this area. There is also a bias in the framing of the book, stemming from my own involvement as an ANC and an anti-war activist during the 1980s; but I hope that this experience has enhanced my understanding of MK. I want to write a popular account which is both a critical, anti-war history and a history that is profoundly empathetic to the experiences of ordinary soldiers fighting for a just cause.

2

# The turn to armed
# struggle, 1960–3

It is hard to find anyone in South Africa today who will argue with conviction that the armed struggle for liberation from apartheid was not justified. This was not always the case, especially among whites. Even so, most South Africans today are grateful that the country did not descend into a full-scale civil war during the apartheid era. Just as there are few who would deny the justice of the liberation struggle, so there are few who would argue that the struggle against apartheid should have 'gone further' and that there would have been a beneficial outcome to a bloody civil war, however revolutionary.

So what started the three-decades-long armed struggle – termed a 'low-intensity war' in the academic literature – between the liberation movement and the apartheid regime? At first glance, it seems quite straightforward. After the introduction of apartheid in 1948, there was a decade of militant yet nonviolent protest and defiance by the ANC and its allies. But when this strategy failed to produce any change of heart on the part of the white government, the ANC began to reconsider its position. The tipping point was provided by the Sharpeville massacre of 1960, when protests against the pass laws were met with brute force by the police: 69 unarmed protesters were shot, many of them in the back as they were fleeing, on 21 March 1960 in an African township near Vereeniging. The government declared a State of Emergency, detained thousands without trial, and banned both the ANC and the PAC (Pan Africanist Congress), a newly formed breakaway from the ANC. Both bodies declared there was no longer any legal space for them to organise nonviolent resistance to apartheid, and set up their armed wings, MK and Poqo respectively.

MK launched its armed struggle on 16 December 1961 with a series of acts of 'symbolic sabotage'; at the same time it distributed a pamphlet announcing MK's formation. As the Manifesto memorably declared: 'The time comes in the life of any nation when there remain only two choices: submit or fight. That time has now come to South Africa.' Despite the accepted wisdom that the turn to armed struggle was obvious, necessary and inevitable, the process was in fact complex and difficult and not uncontested even within the ANC.

There were those within the ANC and its allies, such as Raymond Mhlaba of Port Elizabeth, who had been arguing for some years that the time for armed struggle had come. This conventional wisdom about the inescapability of military resistance was widely held among colonised and oppressed people in the 1960s and 1970s throughout the world. Within South Africa, there were also those who did not think the mass nonviolent protests of the 1950s had been ineffective or exhausted; and there were trade unionists and church leaders who were committed to continuing to build and strengthen their organisations and institutions as sites of opposition to apartheid.

Because of the largely Christian adherence of most ANC members, including its president Albert Luthuli, the formation of MK was not in the beginning carried out under the auspices of the ANC but as a 'people's army at the disposal of the South

African masses', not directly linked to the ANC. Luthuli's stance in fact continues to evoke heated debate. In a radio discussion of a new biography of the Chief in late 2010, listeners who phoned in were incensed that the author, the American Scott Couper, could claim that Luthuli was unable to support the decision to turn to armed struggle. Couper agreed that the argument around the justice of the ANC's turn to armed struggle was convincing: if ever there was a just war, this was it. And yet he argued equally convincingly that while Luthuli understood why other leading figures in the ANC wanted to adopt a strategy of violence, and would not openly criticise it, he could not personally support the decision.

Some ANC activists were also swayed by the Gandhian tradition in South African politics, particularly those of Indian descent who were followers of the Mahatma and his philosophy of nonviolent resistance to oppression. In an ongoing history project on South African war veterans' experiences, one student is examining the way in which Indian MK members from Durban came to terms with the implications of abandoning their Gandhian beliefs and accepting the necessity of violence.

Although the decision in 1960 to engage in armed struggle is, in hindsight at least, not surprising, this did not make it any easier to prosecute successfully. And what followed in the next three decades was no easier for the guerrilla army.

MK was established by a small group of saboteurs of all races recruited from the ANC and its ally the South African Communist Party (SACP). Having been banned by the government since 1950, as a result of which it acquired some experience of underground organisation, the SACP was influential in MK from the beginning owing to its members' technical skills and their revolutionary theory. The initial number of MK recruits was around 250, organised into units of three to four members, groups of which would fall under a Regional Command structure in the main urban centres. Unity in action and nonracialism were emphasised in MK from the beginning. White, coloured and Indian activists from the SACP and other allies of the ANC like the Congress of Democrats, the Coloured People's Organisation and the Indian Congress joined African activists from the ANC and the Congress of Trade Unions.

The first acts of sabotage were planned for 16

December, a day of great symbolic importance in South Africa, celebrated by Afrikaner nationalists as the Day of the Vow or Dingaan's Day to commemorate a Boer victory over Zulu forces at the Battle of Blood River in 1838. MK leadership symbolically turned the defeat of Dingane by the Boers on its head, by launching their campaign against white rule on the same day.

Meanwhile, before the day arrived, a group of MK members was sent to China for training, among them Raymond Mhlaba. Returning in October 1962, he was asked to take over Nelson Mandela's position as Commander-in-Chief of MK, after Mandela had been arrested. It was at the end of 1962 that MK was first referred to as the military wing of the ANC and publicly acknowledged as such.

There are some wonderful accounts of the first MK campaign, the sabotage campaign of 1961–3. Most appear in the biographies or autobiographies of high-profile leaders of the ANC and SACP. In addition to the well-known writings of Nelson Mandela, and those of Govan Mbeki, who wrote extensively about the turn to armed struggle before his death in 2001, one can read (to highlight a few) *Slovo: The Unfinished Autobiography* (1995),

*Hani: A Life Too Short* (2009), Ronnie Kasrils's two entertaining accounts of early MK days in Durban, *Armed and Dangerous* (1993), largely about himself, and *The Unlikely Secret Agent* (2010), about his wife Eleanor's role in MK, and *Raymond Mhlaba's Personal Memoirs* as narrated to Thembeka Mufamadi (2001). Indres Naidoo, Ahmed Kathrada and Mac Maharaj have all documented their experiences as Indian MK members in the 1960s. These writings have been supplemented recently by oral history projects which allow the 'ordinary soldiers' of MK to speak for the first time. The first volume of the SADET history project, *The Road to Democracy in South Africa* (2004), drew extensively on interviews with the 1960s generation in describing the first phase of armed struggle, while *Men of Dynamite* (2009) documented the experiences of the Indian activists from MK units in Johannesburg in the early 1960s.

Some of these first members of MK have described how they were convinced of the need for armed struggle or how they were recruited. Ronnie Kasrils, for example, tells how he joined MK in Durban: 'During July 1961, MP Naicker took me for a walk along the beachfront. He confided that the Movement was about to change its strategy. The government's repressive policies had convinced the leadership that non-violent struggle alone could not bring about change. We were forced to answer the regime's violence with revolutionary violence.' Kasrils then became a member of the Natal Regional Command of MK, working with the trade unionists Curnick Ndlovu, Billy Nair, Eric Mtshali and Bruno Mtolo.

These first MK units engaged in reconnaissance to identify appropriate targets for sabotage and then were confronted with the need to find or make the right kind of explosives. As MK had very limited weaponry or materiel for the sabotage campaign, members experimented with explosives obtained by various ingenious means, such as experimenting with shop-bought chemicals and stealing dynamite from a road construction camp and a quarry. Former soldiers who had fought in the Second World War, including Jack Hodgson in Durban and Harold Strachan in Port Elizabeth, assisted with making explosives. Strachan talks about buying chemicals from a pharmacy and making bombs from scratch.

The accounts of these first amateur attempts at sabotage, told with self-deprecating humour and indicative of fierce commitment, are both amusing and deeply admirable. My personal favourite is Harold Strachan's story in *Make a Skyf, Man!* (2004) of the MK technical committee testing explosives on a remote stretch of coast near Port Elizabeth and blowing up an abandoned seaside toilet to impress Joe Slovo ('Yoshke'). 'We say to all When we raise a fist in the torchlight down there you must start timing seven and a half minutes, and they find this terribly thrilling in a revolutionary sort of way, and we go down and slosh in the glycerine and wave our revolutionary fists with our left fingers over the glass of the torch so as not to make a beam, and walk ewe gerus oh so confidently up the hill to the Olds. At seven minutes Yoshke starts some interminable ideological comment on what's going on, but its probable thirty minutes' duration are interrupted at seven and a half minutes exactly by a low-resonance stunning thud and a sphere of white fire the size of a smallish city hall, and in the middle of it a toilet seat spinning like crazy over the Indian Ocean.'

While the MK sabotage campaign was aimed strictly at installations, and was intended, as Mandela said, to 'bring the regime to its senses before it was too late', it was only the first stage in what was understood by the leadership to be revolutionary warfare. The next phase, Operation Mayibuye, envisaged armed support for a national insurrection, with plans to bring 28,000 anti-personnel mines into the country. Such a strategy, if implemented, would have been a far cry from the selective and symbolic sabotage operations of the first phase. An extract from Operation Mayibuye reads: 'It can now truly be said that very little, if any, scope exists for the smashing of white supremacy other than by means of mass revolutionary action, the main content of which is armed resistance, leading to victory by military means ... We are confident that the masses will respond in overwhelming numbers to a lead which holds out a real possibility of successful armed struggle.'

It was to be another two decades before the 'masses' responded in overwhelming numbers to MK's call to 'make the country ungovernable, make apartheid unworkable'. Yet the threat of revolutionary violence was enough to obtain the conviction of the MK leaders, arrested at Lilliesleaf farm in Rivonia, on charges of high treason in 1963–4. It was the Rivonia Trial and the subsequent imprisonment of most of the MK High Command on Robben Island that brought the early phase of MK activities to an end.

What were the gains and losses arising from this stage of MK's operations? First of all, the strategy of symbolic sabotage was highly effective in conveying a message to the black majority that the time had come to fight the apartheid regime. But, as could perhaps have been anticipated, it did not succeed in 'bringing the government to its senses before it was too late'. Instead, it resulted in a massive repressive backlash of harsh legislation, arrests, torture and political trials, and even executions. In terms of costs in human life and suffering, not one life was lost in the nearly 200 acts of sabotage committed between 1961 and 1964. This was because the targets and the timing of these acts were planned and carried out with considerable care by the amateur cadres. As Mandela stated during the Rivonia Trial, this was definitely not a campaign of terrorism. However, there was an element of luck involved as well: sabotage of a railway line, designed to derail a passenger train, failed; and attacks on beerhalls where there could have been civilian casualties, fortunately resulted in no loss of life.

Despite the policy of not taking lives, two people

were killed by MK members, although not as the result of the acts of sabotage. These actions involved the death of a 14-year-old girl in East London on 11 December 1962, and the killing of Sipho Mange in Port Elizabeth on 12 January 1964. They were met by a predictably harsh response from the South African Police and led in turn to the first executions of MK members.

The stories of the 14-year-old and of Sipho Mange provide some of the first examples of a continuing dilemma that MK would have to confront over the decades. It is a dilemma faced by all underground organisations and guerrilla armies, and is one that often leads to cruelty and tragedy. From the very first acts of sabotage in 1961 it became clear that MK would have problems with infiltration by police spies and betrayal by informers and by those pressed to become state witnesses in trials against former comrades. While MK sabotage actions were clearly targeted at strategic installations, and considerable care was taken not to cause loss of life, it was actions against collaborators that resulted in the first MK deaths.

In the first case, Washington Bongco, the Regional Commander of MK in East London, was involved in an attack on the home of Inkie Domboti Hovi on 11 December 1962. The attack involved the use of petrol bombs and at least one gun. Although Hovi was shot at, he survived, but his niece was burnt to death and his daughter seriously injured. Hovi was considered a collaborator because of his support for the proposed nominal autonomy of the Transkei homeland and for its first head of government, Chief Kaiser Matanzima. While it is unclear whether the MK command at national level sanctioned the attack, the ANC at the time published pamphlets condemning collaboration and the 'traitors' and 'sell-outs' who joined the Transkeian authorities.

In this context, the Eastern Cape diverged from national MK strategy by attacking individuals, often in their homes. Such personal targets made up 21 of the Eastern Cape attacks, the second most frequent category in that region. In the main, the targets were local representatives of Kaiser Matanzima or persons regarded as supporting the Transkei 'homeland', and a few were attacks on the homes of black policemen. According to some reports, MK's national headquarters sent Govan Mbeki to look into the activities of the Eastern Cape region and concluded that Bongco had 'exceeded his authority'.

After his arrest by the police, Bongco was sentenced to death and hanged on 10 December 1964.

The second case involved Sipho Mange, who was shot in the head at his home in Port Elizabeth in January 1963. His assassination had been ordered by the Regional Command of MK, whose four members were Commander Diliza Khayingo, Commissar Vuyisile Mini, Zinakele Mkaba and Kholisile Mdwayi. Of this MK network, the first three, Mini, Khayingo and Mkaba, were executed on 6 November 1964 following their conviction on charges of sabotage and conspiracy to murder. The 'foot soldiers' who carried out the orders, Nolali Petse, Daniel Ndongeni and Samuel Jonas, were sentenced to death on 23 February 1965 and hanged on 9 July 1965. Other MK members were charged with sabotage or with belonging to a banned organisation.

It is common knowledge in the ANC that Mini and his comrades were hanged for the killing of an *impimpi* (spy or police informer) or a 'sell-out'. However, it seems that the distinction was not made at the time – nor was it made subsequently – between different categories of betrayal: informers (those paid by the police for information); agents (spies infiltrated by the police into resistance organisations); collaborators (those who aligned themselves politically with institutions associated with the apartheid regime, such as homeland administrations or Black Local Authorities); and state witnesses (MK or ANC members who agreed to give state evidence – often after torture – in the trial of their comrades). The death of Mange was probably the first case in the operations of MK of the 'ultimate penalty' being imposed for betrayal of the movement. According to the court evidence, Mange was to appear as a state witness at the trial of three other MK members charged for sabotage. It thus appears that he was executed for his intention to betray the organisation by testifying against his comrades. At a later stage, MK adopted a clear policy of assassinating those who turned state witness in political trials, as with Leonard Nkosi in 1977 and Steve Mtshali in 1978.

At the time of the Mange killing, Walter Sisulu, one of the ANC's leaders who was subsequently convicted at the Rivonia Trial, made a statement that local units of MK had to 'take the initiative' in dealing with informers. If this was indeed the policy, it would seem that MK orders at national level were

## Songs of this era

In the 1950s, when the ANC was committed to nonviolent direct action and formed the 'Doctors' Pact' with the leaders of the Natal and Transvaal Indian Congresses, Dr Dadoo and Dr Naicker, there was a song which celebrated this unity and called for volunteers to participate in the campaigns of the movement.

*Yebo, yebo Chief Luthuli, nawe Doctor Naicker, sikhokhele* (Yes, Chief Luthuli, and you Doctor Naicker, we follow you)
*Gcina, gcina amavolontiya, gcina, gcina ama-Afrika* (Keep safe the volunteers, keep safe the people of Africa)

*Amavolontiya*, as they were called, were required to be disciplined and dedicated cadres. There are some who regard the *amavolontiya* as the forerunners of MK cadres, because of their discipline. This is debatable: there is no reason why nonviolent activists cannot be equally disciplined and prepared to sacrifice, as in the Gandhian tradition of nonviolent resistance. With the first trained MK soldiers in exile named the Luthuli

Detachment, the songs sung in the 1950s by the volunteers were equally appropriate for the new 'soldiers of Luthuli'.

*Amajoni, amajoni, amajoni, amajoni* (Soldiers)
*uMandela ufuna amajoni, amajoni ase-Afrika* (Mandela wants soldiers, soldiers of Africa)
*Singamasoja, soja kaMandela/Luthuli* (We are the soldiers of Mandela/Luthuli)
*Singamasoja kaMandela*
*Lapho, lapho, lapho siyakhona* (Where we are going)
*Thina silindel' inkululeko* (We are anticipating freedom)
*Thula mama, thula mama* (Quiet Mama)
*Ngoba thina, singamasoja kaLuthuli noMandela* (We are the soldiers of Luthuli and Mandela)
*Singabafana baloMkhonto weSizwe* (We are the men of MK)
*Singamasoja kaJoe Slovo nakaTambo* (We are the soldiers of Joe Slovo and of Tambo)

But this time they were real soldiers, carrying guns; and nobody will ever know how Chief Luthuli would have felt about these songs.

'deliberately vague' at this early stage, allowing for people within Regional Command structures to give orders for assassination.

This was an issue which plagued MK in later years, when its High Command was located far away in other countries, and struggled to maintain lines of communication with units or cells operating in townships around South Africa. In many cases, the unit commanders were given a high degree of initiative and discretion in making decisions about targets. Peter Harris's account in his book *In a Different Time* (2008) of the decisions regarding targets made by the MK unit called the 'Delmas Four' provides a good example of this. Such problematic 'on-the-ground' decisions about what constituted a legitimate or 'hard' target, and what did not, were often left to junior MK cadres. It goes without saying that the issue of traitors and spies was even more tricky.

The story of Vuyisile Mini and his comrades is a good example of just how difficult and problematic such issues were in the early days of MK. Indeed, the story is more complicated than the public version of events would allow. Kholisile Mdwayi, the fourth member of the Regional Command, was arrested in

June 1963 and became the key state witness in the trial of Mini, Khayingo and Mkaba, where he gave devastating evidence. Though there is no evidence to suggest Mdwayi was an agent provocateur, what is apparent is that one of those who gave the order to kill a state witness then underwent a change of heart and became a state witness himself.

While it is not disputed that Sipho Mange was killed on instructions of MK, it seems that he was to some extent an innocent victim. There is no evidence that he was a police informer. He was not even an MK member, but an ANC volunteer who was picked up by the police in Kwazakhele in Port Elizabeth, and tortured – as were many others – into agreeing to give evidence against his comrades. Some have also asserted that the 'foot soldiers' who were ordered to carry out the killing were framed and were not actually involved in Mange's murder. While the decision to kill Mange was made by the Regional Command, including Mdwayi, the consequence was that the whole Regional Command became implicated in an action that ultimately led to their destruction.

Whatever the truth of the matter, it is clear that this tragedy illustrates one of the terrible challenges faced by MK from the very beginning of its operations: the problem of infiltration, of informers or people who had been 'turned' by the authorities. Many more were to die, whether innocent or guilty, because of such infiltration.

Vuyisile Mini, the best-known of the six MK members from Port Elizabeth who were executed in 1964, became the first MK martyr. Mini was a brave and colourful man, a trade union organiser and a marvellous singer, who composed freedom songs and sang them in a deep bass voice. His most famous song was 'Bhasopha, nants' indod' emnyama, Verwoerd' (Watch out, here is the black man, Verwoerd!). He is said to have gone to the gallows singing. His comrades Khayingo and Mkaba were also immortalised in poetry and song. The ANC Freedom Choir performed and recorded these songs and distributed them around the world and they were often played in MK camps.

After 1994, the remains of the six executed MK members from Port Elizabeth were disinterred and reburied at Emlotheni Square in New Brighton township, where there is now a memorial park and where their contribution to history is remembered. From the engraving on the 'wall of remembrance', it could be imagined that the six MK members had died as soldiers in battle. The truth was that the members of the Regional Command were executed because they had ordered the death of an alleged collaborator.

# 3

# The Wankie and Sipolilo
# campaigns, 1967–8

Those who left the country for military training in
the early 1960s, including the young Chris Hani,
who was later to become MK Chief of Staff, did
not have an easy time of it. After receiving military
training in various countries, including Algeria and
China, many ended up living in harsh conditions
in the Kongwa camp in Tanzania. Most believed
that the revolutionary war planned by MK would
take place in the immediate future, and expected
victory before the end of the decade. Their hopes of
rapid deployment into South Africa were, however,
disappointed, and many complained bitterly of
languishing in camps while the ANC leadership
engaged in diplomatic and fundraising activities
around the world. In 1966 a group of dissatisfied
MK members, including Chris Hani, drafted a
memorandum of their grievances and expressed

their frustration at not being deployed to fight.

The problem for MK's High Command was to infiltrate guerrillas back into South Africa. At that time South Africa was surrounded by a cordon sanitaire of neighbouring states that had not yet achieved independence from colonial rule or imperial overlordship: South West Africa (Namibia) had become a fifth province of South Africa; Angola and Mozambique were still colonies of Portugal; and Rhodesia (Zimbabwe) was in the hands of a white minority government that had declared its independence from the UK. In all of these countries, the first stirrings of the turn to armed struggle by indigenous liberation movements were being felt. As for the three former British protectorates of Bechuanaland (Botswana), Basutoland (Lesotho) and Swaziland, these were economically dominated by South Africa, which used its superior power to lean on them and prevent their being used as bases for MK.

As a way of creating an entry route for MK guerrillas into South Africa through Rhodesia, the ANC established a formal alliance with the Zimbabwe African People's Union (ZAPU) of Joshua Nkomo, which was supported by the Soviet

Union. This step was also in line with the adoption, by MK's liberation movement allies in other African countries, of the strategy of rural guerrilla warfare. The alliance between the ANC and ZAPU led to the activation of some of the newly trained MK members in military operations in cooperation with ZIPRA guerrillas in the north-west of Rhodesia. The attempt to create a passage through Rhodesia into South Africa by fighting with ZIPRA against combined Rhodesian and South African forces was both heroic and disastrous. Those who survived the Wankie and Sipolilo campaigns, as they became known, were hailed as *mgwenya*, having crossed the Zambezi River under the command of Charles Ngwenya. (Coincidentally, *umgwenya* is also the word for crocodile in Siswati; some MK cadres were literally eaten by crocodiles inhabiting the rivers they had to cross.)

What was it like to be a guerrilla soldier fighting in the southern African bush in the 1960s? As in all forms of warfare, it was desperately hard for those who were tasked with the fighting. But this was not the Soviet Union, where soldiers froze to death; it was Africa. The suffering experienced was the harshest imaginable, including lack of drinking water and lack of food. MK soldiers describe how they had to share the muddy drinking water from rivers with elephants. They also describe walking for hundreds of kilometres in the sweltering heat, or walking through the night while wild animals hunted nearby.

Perhaps the most horrifying experience was that of the unit attacked by a group of hungry crocodiles. According to the MK commander Eric Mtshali, a group of 12 MK and ZAPU cadres under his command were instructed to cross the Zambezi to rescue a section of the Luthuli Detachment that had been surrounded by Rhodesian forces. The group crossed the mighty river at night in three small dinghies. When the commander's boat reached the opposite bank, and he and his group were clambering out, they noticed that one of the other two boats had capsized. 'In no time the water around it turned red with blood. Two comrades were swimming frantically towards the shore. They never made any sound and, up to this day, I do not know why they never screamed. Two others had disappeared without a trace. All we could see was a pack of crocodiles fighting over their limbs. It was a very disturbing sight, and we were all taken aback and furious to lose soldiers in that way. It was a very demoralising experience.'

Notwithstanding the hardships borne, the MK guerrillas did gain valuable experience of the reality of warfare. They engaged the enemy in a series of battles, between August 1967 and May 1968. From all accounts they fought bravely and intelligently, and the Rhodesian and South African forces confronting them were surprised both by their sophisticated weaponry and by their clever battle tactics. There were casualties on both sides.

One vivid account of an engagement is given by 'Comrade Rogers', who fought in the battle of Nyatuwe River, and wrote about it for the 1986 'Souvenir Issue' of *Dawn*, the MK journal. 'In a few seconds I was up, took my bag and gun, told Masimini and Sibanyoni to follow me and ordered Kid to cover me. On the way I met Zami, who was alone manning another position, firing at the enemy. The fire that side was very heavy. I thought the enemy could be trying to make a breakthrough from that side. I instructed Sibanyoni to take position besides Zami with his LMG [light machine gun] and ordered Zami to cease fire and wait till the enemy was 50 m away. I told him that the day was still young and we had to be careful not to exhaust our supplies of ammunition. "Our survival depends on our accuracy," I said. I also gave them their sectors of fire.

'Suddenly the enemy burst out from the trees and there were helicopters hovering over us. We took positions, I and Masimini, joined by Sharp. We were five. None opened fire. The enemy was firing from the hip, rushing towards us. When I estimated they were 50 m and their fire was already pinning us down, I replied with my sub-machine gun.

'Hell broke loose. We concentrated our fire where the enemy had taken cover and we are certain we injured and killed many. I signalled to Zami and Masimini to cease fire. We waited for about three minutes during which the fire from the enemy had subsided. I retreated with both Zami and Masimini. I was going to collect the third LMG, which I gave to Zami. My main worry was the hillock. If we could allow the enemy to capture it, our position would be very precarious. We came out of the bush and ran towards the hillock. When we were at the foot of the hillock a helicopter appeared. It opened fire at us with its 12.7mm machine gun. We ran back to the bush and took cover …'

The description of this particular battle continues. After further conflicts, they were overpowered by the enemy, by which time 'only seven of us were remaining, five ZAPU comrades, myself and Bothwell'. All were captured, and the two MK soldiers were sentenced to death. Their sentences – along with those of other MK cadres captured in Rhodesia – were commuted to life imprisonment, and they were released in 1980, after the Patriotic Front (ZANU–ZAPU) victory in the first democratic elections in Zimbabwe.

The power of this account lies in the detail given of the experience of commanding a military operation, the commander thinking tactically under extreme duress and putting into practice all that was learnt in training. It also tells of acts of great courage on the part of highly motivated soldiers. But it must be remembered that *Dawn* was written to inspire MK cadres and others who might join MK: it did not recount the terror experienced during battle, nor the ignoble or humiliating acts that soldiers would rather forget.

The Wankie and Sipolilo campaigns are undoubtedly significant in the history of MK as a military organisation, as they represented the first engagement in 'conventional' guerrilla warfare as distinct from symbolic sabotage. At this stage, MK expected that its strategy would be primarily that of protracted rural guerrilla warfare, similar to the one FRELIMO had engaged in in Mozambique: a lengthy process in which the guerrillas gradually obtained control of remote rural areas, won over the inhabitants and set up 'liberated zones' from where they could launch operations into the urban and industrial centres of the country.

According to Howard Barrell, who wrote one of the first serious analyses of MK, 'The ANC's actual approach was that armed activity was the only significant way to procure military advance. The hope, implicit in the design of the campaigns, was that armed activity by a small MK force was capable of drawing the population into, and eventually detonating, all-round political-military revolt against the state.' He suggests that this 'campaign design' and its underlying strategy were influenced by the success of the Cuban Revolution and by Che Guevara's 'foci' or 'detonator' strategy. Though the ANC leadership denied this at the Morogoro national conference in 1969, a similar strategy was employed just a few years later, in the *Aventura* episode (which is recounted later).

There are other assessments of the ANC's campaigns of the late 1960s. One criticism is that the military strategy adopted was inappropriate for southern Africa. The ANC and ZAPU mechanically applied the doctrine of 'mobile warfare', using columns of 30 or more men, which made their presence almost impossible to disguise. While the actions of the Luthuli Detachment in Zimbabwe were undeniably heroic, providing an example for the next generation of MK soldiers to follow, the Wankie and Sipolilo campaigns did not offer military answers to the question of how to engage the apartheid state. Some argue that the campaigns were a plain military disaster, with a high loss of life and no military gains for MK. Others argue that the campaign was only embarked on to deflect pressure on the leadership from restless MK members stuck in the Kongwa camp in Tanzania. Stephen Ellis and Tsepo Sechaba, in *Comrades against Apartheid*, wrote that 'Armies, especially those motivated by revolutionary idealism, exist to fight'. The most cynical critics of the campaign argue that the MK members who had 'mutinied' were sent into battle to fulfil their demands or even to get them out of the way on a 'suicide mission'. Yet another criticism is that the guerrillas were ill prepared, relying on ZAPU's weak contacts with the local population, having done inadequate reconnaissance of the terrain, and consequently having insufficient food and ammunition to remain in Rhodesia and make their way to South Africa.

In both these campaigns, there were significant casualties inflicted on the Rhodesian forces. But the casualties among MK members were even higher. Nearly 50 MK cadres lost their lives in the Wankie and Sipolilo campaigns, in what Paul Trewhela calls a 'disastrous fiasco'. The strategic objective of creating a path home – 'the corridor must be opened at all costs,' said MK Masimini, who lost his life after being injured in the battle described above – was not achieved.

According to Ellis and many other commentators, it was a 'military defeat with a positive symbolic value'. For both ZAPU and the ANC, the campaigns taught them 'the folly of engaging a better-equipped army head-on in the conventional manner then favoured by the Soviet instructors'. The historian Luli Callinicos summarises the significance of the 1967–8 campaigns as follows: 'Historically, Wankie came to symbolise the problem that was increasingly to bedevil the ANC's armed wing. Despite repeated attempts to return home in large numbers, this was never achieved.'

All the same, the symbolic value of the campaigns was much drawn upon officially by the ANC in numerous commemorations and acknowledgements, at which those who had taken part in the bush war in Rhodesia were hailed as 'torchbearers of the revolution'. According to Oliver Tambo, president of the ANC in exile, when speaking in 1986 on the anniversary of the founding of MK: 'Wankie revived the spirits of our people inside our country, restored courage in the face of repression and revitalised the revolution!'

But the kind of warfare displayed in the Wankie and Sipolilo campaigns – indeed, the kind of rural guerrilla warfare fought by local liberation movements in Zimbabwe, Mozambique and Angola – would hardly be a feature of MK's later military actions in South Africa. Though there were to be similar confrontations in Angola in the 1970s, and one or two such encounters in rural South Africa, such as the Battle of Mutale River in the northern Transvaal in 1988, these encounters were few and far between.

The Wankie and Sipolilo campaigns were the largest-scale military conflicts that MK engaged in throughout its 30-year history; and they were very costly in terms of loss of combatants to capture, imprisonment and injury, not to mention loss of life itself. But were smaller units, infiltrating into urban environments, to fare any better? Only the next two decades would tell. Meanwhile, the hopes of a quick return and a rapid revolutionary seizure of state power were once again put on the back burner.

4

# Struggling to get home, 1969–84

Following the Wankie and Sipolilo campaigns,
the ANC held a decisive national conference at
Morogoro in Tanzania in 1969 to deal with the
unprecedented level of criticism and dissatisfaction
within the organisation. Survivors of the Rhodesian
campaigns were openly critical of the leadership;
those in MK camps expecting deployment in South
Africa were tired of waiting. After much discussion
the conference adopted a 'Strategy and Tactics'
document in which it outlined the way ahead for the
organisation, focusing on a shift in strategy to rural
guerrilla warfare prosecuted 'outside the enemy
strongholds in the cities, in the vast stretches of our
countryside'.

This redirection was guided by current thinking
in revolutionary circles about overthrowing
authoritarian or colonial governments through the

mobilisation of rural peasants as the shock troops of revolution. In South Africa the possibility of such a strategy had seemed confirmed and anticipated by rural uprisings during the 1950s in such diverse areas as Sekhukhuneland and especially Pondoland, where the Mpondo Revolt had required the intervention of the South African army to put down in 1959. And yet the fact is that rural guerrilla warfare was never successfully implemented by MK.

Through the first half of the 1970s, MK experimented, largely without success, with ways of infiltrating combatants into South Africa or recruiting local people into underground units. In the early 1970s, a number of people, mainly white communists, were recruited and trained by Ronnie Kasrils, based in London, to set up underground cells and distribute pamphlets and detonate pamphlet bombs in the main urban centres so as to keep the name of the ANC alive. One of these recruits, Raymond Suttner, has written a moving account of his exploits and of the time he spent in prison after capture and torture. Despite the importance of such tactics in maintaining the public presence of the ANC within the country, there was little success achieved in establishing military networks for MK.

The insurrectionary theories popular in those days were expected to generate quick results, but in the case of South Africa this was easier theorised than put into practice.

Given the difficulties of infiltrating combatants, MK began to organise regional commands in each of the 'forward areas' of Swaziland, Lesotho and Botswana, the former British protectorates on (and, in the case of Lesotho, within) South Africa's borders. From here, MK units entered the country, setting up underground networks and laying the basis for military operations. Some of South Africa's best-known political leaders were involved in attempts to establish underground networks in South Africa in the mid-1970s. Among them were former president Thabo Mbeki and current president Jacob Zuma. Both were based in the Swaziland 'forward area'. Zuma's biographer Jeremy Gordin notes that Mbeki was Zuma's commander and actually trained Zuma in the use of firearms. Infiltration and betrayal led, however, to the decimation of these units. As Gordin remarks, 'the security police seemed to be ahead of the game'. One of the units linked to the Swaziland network was nevertheless successful in late 1976 in blowing up a railway line in the eastern Transvaal, resulting in a skirmish with the South African Police. Mosima 'Tokyo' Sexwale, another cadre from the Swaziland forward area, was among those arrested and charged in 1977 for MK activities.

It was in the late 1970s that MK actually did manage to 'come back inside' and restart military operations within South Africa, though on a very limited scale. There were only ten to twelve incidents in each year from 1977 to 1979. The most famous of these was the Goch Street shootout in Johannesburg in 1977. In this incident two civilians became victims of an 'unplanned panic reaction' when an MK unit was tracked down and cornered by the police. Of the members of this unit, George 'Lucky' Mazibuko escaped, while the two others, Monty Motlaung and Solomon Mahlangu, were captured. Motlaung was so severely beaten by his captors that he suffered brain damage and was unable to stand trial. The remaining member, Solomon Mahlangu, had not actually fired a shot during the encounter, but he stood trial nevertheless and was sentenced to death. Mahlangu's statement in the dock before he was hanged on 6 April 1979 was widely repeated afterwards and ensured that his bravery and sacrifice became fixed in the minds of young black South

Africans: 'Do not worry about me. But worry about those who are suffering. My blood will nourish the tree that will bear the fruits of freedom. Tell my people that I love them. They must continue the fight.' With these dramatic words, the 23-year-old became the first MK martyr since Vuyisile Mini. He has since been commemorated in Solomon Mahlangu Square in Mamelodi, Johannesburg, and a play has been written about him called *Kalushi: The Story of Solomon Mahlangu.*

Nevertheless, the Goch Street incident was not typical of MK operations and was regarded by MK as an 'unplanned' action resulting in civilian casualties. The MK modus operandi in this period was to send a small number of cadres over the border into the urban areas, in order to select targets. Most of these were government buildings: police stations, railway lines and Bantu Affairs Administration Board offices (which administered control of the urban black population through the hated passes). Attacks on these sites were termed 'pot-boiling' operations, designed to keep awareness of MK alive, to link up with local struggles or grievances where possible, and to maintain pressure on the regime. Some of those attacked, usually with guns, were individuals (either security force members or state witnesses) targeted for assassination. Lastly, there were 'skirmishes' with police, confrontations that occurred either when MK members ambushed the police or, more commonly, when the police had tracked down members of a unit.

This pattern of operation was to continue through the next decade, with some exceptions. One was the rural landmine campaign of 1985–7, which is described later. The other was a number of attacks on civilian targets towards the end of the 1980s, when MK actions reached their peak.

At this early stage, however, the instructions given to units were to make their way into urban areas and use the explosive devices they had at their disposal to attack selected targets. The further the urban areas were from the borders, the more difficult it was for the units to sustain their security and anonymity. One little-known MK hero from this period was Makwezi McDonald Mtulu, who died in Port Elizabeth in 1978.

For those unfamiliar with the geography of South Africa, it should be explained that Port Elizabeth is on the southern coast of the African continent, very far from the borders of South Africa with Botswana, Zimbabwe or Mozambique. The closest international border is Lesotho, a tiny and impoverished landlocked country, where a forward area called 'The Island' was established in the late 1970s, after the ANC's Revolutionary Council had been restructured. At the same time the ANC had set up an Internal Political Reconstruction Committee (IPRC) with the idea of rebuilding the underground networks and linking military and political work. Regional IPRCs were also established in Botswana, Swaziland, Mozambique and, most importantly for the Eastern Cape, in Lesotho. The IPRC in Lesotho was led by Chris Hani and Lambert Moloi and included Linda Mti. At the same time there was a military Joint Command based in Lesotho to coordinate MK actions in the Eastern Cape.

Although few in number, explosions in urban areas in 1978 and 1979 provided an indication that MK was beginning to infiltrate saboteurs, explosives and weapons back into the country. The first two explosions took place in Port Elizabeth. One of the bombs went off outside the Bantu Affairs Administration Board offices in New Brighton. One civilian was killed and three injured. The other device, described as a 'parcel bomb', exploded in

Cawood Street, at the heart of the commercial downtown centre of North End, on 8 March 1978. The person carrying the bomb was blown to pieces and one other person was slightly injured when windows were shattered and cars damaged. The MK cadre who died in the blast, presumably when his bomb exploded prematurely, was labelled in the press as 'Port Elizabeth's first urban terrorist'. His name was Makwezi McDonald Mtulu, and he was said to have gone into exile in 1972 for military training.

What is disturbing about this incident is that it was not the only occasion that an MK cadre died when his own bomb exploded. In Port Elizabeth a similar incident occurred in January 1983 when Petros Bokala (MK James) was also killed by his own bomb outside the offices of the Port Elizabeth Community Council in New Brighton. There are also unconfirmed reports that in 1981 yet another MK cadre died when his bomb exploded prematurely at a bus terminus in the nearby city of East London. These deaths could indicate one of two things: either the MK cadres' training in the use of explosives was inadequate and they made fatal errors in handling their weaponry; or that MK had been infiltrated and their weapons tampered with, either at source or once they had arrived at their destination.

In the late 1970s, the fear of terrorism was great worldwide: the activities of the Baader-Meinhof gang in Germany and the kidnapping and assassination of the Italian premier Aldo Mori were splashed across newspapers. While MK took great pains to distinguish itself from terrorist organisations and to present itself as a legitimate and disciplined guerrilla army, the apartheid regime and many of its allies in the West were quick to classify MK cadres as 'terrorists'. Incidents like the Silverton bank siege in Pretoria in 1980 and the bombing of the South African Air Force Headquarters, also in Pretoria, in 1983 were to reinforce this perception.

Like the Goch Street shootout in 1977, the Silverton bank siege was an unplanned and uncharacteristic action. (It was also the only case in which MK members took hostages.) As controversial was the deliberate placing of a car bomb outside the South African Air Force (SAAF) Headquarters building in Church Street, in central Pretoria, in 1983. The bomb killed the two cadres who planted it, indicating that it had exploded prematurely; it also killed 19 others, 11 of whom were employees of the SAAF, and wounded over 200 more people. The attack resulted in public accusations that the ANC was a terrorist organisation. It was unfortunately also a precedent for things to come: the Magoo's Bar bomb in Durban in 1985, the Ellis Park rugby stadium bomb in 1988, and bombs placed in public dustbins and Wimpy Bars countrywide in 1987–9.

The Church Street bombing is perhaps the most interesting operation, as it was defended as an attack on a legitimate military target by MK leaders and other analysts. The ANC claimed that 11 of the 19 people killed were 'airforce officers' and hence 'legitimate targets'. On the other hand, those who condemned the attack argued that typists and other office workers, even if employed by the Air Force, could not be classified as enemy personnel. The defence used by Aboobaker Ismail, MK Special Operations head, who masterminded the operation, was that the civilian deaths caused during the bombing were a form of 'collateral damage' – an expression used by military forces to describe 'unavoidable' civilian casualties that occur in the course of legitimate military operations. When he testified to the Truth and Reconciliation Commission (TRC) about this incident, he used the bombing of Dresden by the British as a justification. In one of the most moving cases of reconciliation dealt with by the Commission, Neville Clarence, who had been blinded in the blast, publicly forgave Ismail.

Many years later, just before MK was disbanded, Joe Modise, Commander-in-Chief of MK, still felt compelled to explain that the Church Street bomb had gone off prematurely. 'Mr Modise said MK regretted the loss of civilian life in the blast and reiterated it was aimed at the "top brass". Mr Modise conceded, however, there might have been the "odd member who over-stepped his brief" and might have been involved in acts of urban terrorism. He concluded, "the signals were very clear from Lusaka [the ANC/MK headquarters during the years of exile] that we are fighting the regime and not the people".'

More successful as military operations were the blowing up of the SASOL oil refinery in June 1980, when damage of R58 million was caused, with not a single injury. This dramatic act of sabotage of a strategic installation is wonderfully depicted in Shawn Slovo's film *Catch a Fire* (2006). The 1982 sabotage of the Koeberg nuclear power station outside Cape Town was even more daring; again, extensive damage was caused, but with no injuries or loss of life. The potential hazards of destroying a nuclear power station were thankfully not realised. Other attacks such as that made on the Voortrekkerhoogte military base of the South African Defence Force in 1981 were similarly impressive in their careful planning, use of inside intelligence, and good handling of sophisticated explosives. Loss of life was minimal. Most of these operations were carried out by MK's Special Operations Unit, which was formed in 1979, in order to return to the strategy of symbolic sabotage, raising the profile of the ANC and inspiring the masses. The 'hit and run' operations of the Special Operations Unit became legendary and are well known. They found an echo in the song, popular in the South African townships, by Abdullah Ibrahim: 'Hit and run, hit and run / Freedom comes from the barrel of a gun.'

One of the more colourful episodes in the history of MK's operations was the attempt in the early 1970s to dispatch a boat, the *Aventura*, from Somalia and land a force of 25 MK soldiers on the Pondoland coast of the Transkei. This ambitious scheme to create a way home and incite an insurrection was reminiscent of an incident in the Cuban Revolution, when followers of Fidel Castro used an old boat, the *Granma*, in 1956 to convey themselves to Cuba. While not immediately successful, it marked the prelude to Castro's triumphant march into Havana a mere two years later, when he overthrew the corrupt and weak dictatorship of Batista. But the apartheid regime was neither weak nor corrupt in this way, and, having captured some MK soldiers who had been infiltrated and obtaining information from them through torture, forced the actual landing of *Aventura* to be aborted. In South Africa, popular photo-comic stories were published in the *Grensvegter* series depicting the 'communist threat' posed by an attempt to infiltrate guerrillas on a yacht. What the *Aventura* episode indicated was that MK was unlikely to seize state power by adopting the *focismo* of Che Guevara, in terms of which a small group of revolutionaries would incite the masses to insurrection.

In fact, popular unrest and civil revolt within South Africa came about largely independent of the ANC's or MK's actions. Beginning in Durban in 1973 a wave of strikes involving the new black trade unions swept through the urban industrial centres of the country. Though underground members of the South African Congress of Trade Unions (SACTU), the 'labour wing' of the liberation movement and a formal ally of the ANC, did play a part in the development of the independent black labour movement, their role was not uncontroversial. Some left-wing members of the ANC, headed by Martin Legassick, criticised SACTU and the ANC for using nascent black trade unions as recruitment organs for MK, rather than seeing their inherent revolutionary value in building working-class organisation inside South Africa. For their pains Legassick and several colleagues in the Marxist Workers' Tendency were dismissed from the ANC.

More so than the worker strikes, the 1976 Soweto students' uprising burst onto the South African political stage and caught both the ANC and the apartheid government by surprise. The uprising – in which the ANC underground was noticeable for its lack of involvement – spread like wildfire across the country, giving expression to the anger and frustration of a new generation of urban black youth. When the authorities reacted with brute force, the result was that thousands of young people fled into exile, and many of them joined MK. They were drafted into MK's second formation, the June 16 Detachment. Few of them knew anything of the Congress tradition embodied in such figures as Albert Luthuli. What political consciousness they had developed was acquired through the Black Consciousness Movement; their activist experience was of being shot at by police in the streets; and they were aggressive in their desire to return to South Africa and confront the 'Boers' with weapons. Few of them, however, were to achieve their aim of doing so.

An excellent account of this generation of MK recruits and of the way MK transformed their lives is given by James Ngculu in his book *The Honour to Serve* (2009). They were joined by others fleeing the country throughout the 1980s, especially after 1985–6 when South Africa was gripped by civil insurrection. Those who were already activists in the townships and had to leave the country under pressure, and those who left with a conscious desire to join MK and henceforth remain in exile, were termed to have 'skipped' the country. In some townships the term *amany'amazwe* ('other worlds' or 'other countries') was used as a euphemism for exile. In the words of one of the most beautiful MK songs of the time:

*Sizobashiy' abazali* (We are leaving our parents)

*Siya … kwamany' amazwe* (We are going to other worlds/countries)

*Lapha kungazi ubaba nomama* (Going where our father and mother don't know)

*Silandel' inkululeko* (We are following freedom)

*Hayi amabhulu* (No, these Boers)

*Asithatha phi isibind' esingako* (Where do they get the courage/the arrogance)

*Sokuthath' i-Afrika, ayenz' eyawo* (To take Africa, and make it theirs)

*Sizothath' izwelethu, alenz' elawo* (We will take our country, and make it our own)

The tragedy of this situation was that the desire for heroic sacrifice often meant unspeakable loss for families, who did not hear from their sons (or daughters) sometimes for a decade or more, sometimes never again. And those who left with a burning desire to fight for the freedom of their people, usually did not get to engage in combat at all. In some cases they did not return from exile. Though most were later accounted for by the ANC, for some there is no record or explanation of what happened to them.

Those sent to the MK camps in Angola were desperate to come home and fight. The select few chosen for operations inside South Africa were the object of great envy. As in most situations of warfare, much of the soldiers' time was spent waiting. Welile Bottoman (MK Webster), in his autobiographical account of his experiences as an MK soldier in Angola in the 1980s, writes eloquently about the life of young exiles: 'Ours was a displacement and a dissolution that seared the soul and sucked our spirit.'

For new recruits, the first six months of their lives as MK recruits consisted of basic training. Tsepe Motumi, who has made a study of MK, gives a summary of the training received in the Angolan camps, where the majority of MK cadres were trained in the period between 1976 and 1988. He describes the general training in these words:

- Firearms training concentrated on the use of rifles, especially AK47s and other rifles that are standard SADF/SAP issue, like the R1 and R4. Training was also provided in pistol shooting as well as the maintenance of weapons in general. Training was given in the use of both offensive and defensive hand grenades and rocket-propelled grenades.

- Engineering instruction focused on the use of Soviet explosives, including training in limpet, anti-personnel and land mines.

- Some artillery training provided on the 82mm mortar, as well as the Grad-P or 122mm rocket launcher.

- Map reading, concentrating specifically on topographic maps and navigation. Training in drawing sketches of specific locations was given to enable cadres to sketch targets for attack or the specific location of dead-letter boxes (DLBs) containing armaments or leaflets. The subject also assisted in establishing locations where land mines were planted.

- Physical training combined with tactics, which dealt mainly with fitness and

overcoming obstacles on a mock battle
course or strip.

• Military combat work focused mainly
on aspects of intelligence and counter-
intelligence, and the theory of revolution,
which included the building of a
revolutionary and a political army. The
purpose of the course was to teach cadres how
to work in secret and to create underground
structures. Successful completion of the
course was compulsory for those being
deployed in South Africa.

Other forms of training included marching drill,
first aid, communications (using military equipment
as well as secret communication methods), and
political instruction (on topics of ANC history,
South African history, international politics and
Marxist-Leninism). For specialist training, MK
soldiers were sent, in addition to the Soviet Union
and East Germany, to countries like Yugoslavia,
Hungary, Bulgaria and Cuba.

The highlight of the training seems to have been
the young cadres' introduction to guns, as Bottoman

remarks: 'For the group, the important development was our introduction to firearms. It was by the power of the gun our chieftaincies and lands were wrested from our control. It was by the power of the gun the imposed white government kept its rule over us. We believed that with machine guns in our hands the country would be returned to us.

'To our minor disappointment, it turned out that, in our case, guns were not just about vindictive shooting of our oppressors. There were ballistics and war theories that we had to learn before touching the machine guns. Some of us grew sullen, like children who had been promised ice-cream only to be told of the theory of ice, ice-making and food entertainment.'

The bitter reality was that the majority of those who went into exile and received military training were never deployed in South Africa. More died from natural causes – usually malaria – or accidents in the Angolan camps than in combat. Fifty comrades committed suicide. Life in the Angolan camps was miserable, characterised by extreme conditions of heat and deprivation, discomfort, disease, poor diet and strict discipline.

Bottoman writes of the intense frustration felt by

young cadres at not being deployed in South Africa, while the struggle was intensifying in the townships during the 1980s. 'The underlying complaint was that we left the country to get arms and fight the regime. Instead we found ourselves as spectators and cheerleaders of the revolution that continued inside the country. Young boys and girls whose age we were before leaving the country continued to arm themselves with stones, whilst we, fully armed and trained, debated the advisability of supporting mass action with arms. At night we slept with AK rifles tucked between our thighs. Had we taken AKs for wives?' he asks plaintively in his memoir, *The Making of an MK Cadre.*

Meanwhile, in the dusty townships of South Africa, thousands of youths engaged in simultaneous 'toyi-toyi' dances in simulation of the military training that MK soldiers underwent, which they had in turn learned from ZIPRA cadres in Zimbabwe. The following song was sung at the time of the ANC's call for a year of 'Unity in Action' in 1982:

*Ngawo lonyaka womanyano* (This is the year of unity)

*S'khokhele Tambo* (We follow Tambo)

*Ngebhazuka nemotha ne-AK* (With bazookas and mortars and AK47s)

*S'khokhele Tambo* (We follow Tambo)

The youth in the townships energetically enacted the firing of AKs, the throwing of grenades, and the shoulder-high carrying of RPG7s accompanied by a *whoosh!* as they launched their deadly grenades. Incredible ingenuity was displayed in making replicas of such weapons from wood and pieces of scrap metal. Yet very few of the enormous number of real weapons that MK had at its disposal were ever used in battle or made their way into South Africa. Those who had the bazookas and the AKs were thousands of kilometres away from the townships, unable to bring their weapons into the arena of struggle and 'arm the masses' with them.

It is ironic to observe that while MK was being sung about and lionised by the mass movement, which was growing into an enormously powerful force within South Africa, MK itself was going through what was probably its worst crisis in all the years of exile. Frustrated at not being able to get back home, the discipline of cadres in the Angolan camps began to fall apart. From the late 1970s, the MK camps in Angola went through great difficulties. The poisoning of cadres in 1978, followed by the bombing of the Nova Catengue camp by the South African Defence Force (SADF) in 1979, and the subsequent uncovering of a network of infiltrators in 1981, brought MK leaders to the realisation that security in the camps left a lot to be desired. The result was that under the headship of Mzwai Piliso, the Department of Intelligence and Security (known also as Mbokodo, 'the grinding stone'), which had been formed in 1969, was considerably strengthened. MK personnel, who had been sent for training in Eastern Europe and the Soviet Union, returned to strengthen Mbokodo, but ended up in many cases abusing their powers over other young cadres in the camps. In 1979 the ANC set up a prison camp in Angola, the Morris Seabelo Rehabilitation Centre, commonly known as Quatro (Number Four).

The frustrations and deprivation experienced by young cadres, combined with the infiltration of enemy agents, led to mutinies in the camps of Viana and Pango in 1984. The mutinies, known as Mkatashingo or Mkatashiya, a Kimbundu (Angolan) term, according to James Ngculu, meaning 'demonised', were tragic events resulting in the deaths of a number of MK soldiers and the execution of others. Those who fell foul of Mbokodo were subsequently confined in Quatro, sometimes for many years, without trial, in the harshest of conditions.

At the same time, MK found its area of operations circumscribed when the Mozambique government was forced to sign the Nkomati Peace Accord in 1984 under immense pressure from South Africa. It is said that President Samora Machel told O.R. Tambo, ANC president, of the Accord with tears streaming down his face. The implications for MK were grave: with the removal of MK bases from Mozambique, the Swaziland forward area was in effect cut off.

Oliver Tambo was the person who held the movement together in its darkest hours of exile. The PAC had split apart in exile and never really recovered from the stresses of that period. Other movements, allies of the ANC, including the PLO and the IRA, also suffered debilitating splits. While the Mkatashingo mutinies were certainly a serious sign of dissatisfaction and dissension, the ANC leadership was able to assert control of the situation. The mutineers were arrested; some were executed;

others were held in detention in the Quatro camp. The leadership took measures to rectify the unstable situation: grievances of MK members were addressed – at least in part – at the ANC's Kabwe conference in 1985 and, after the unbanning of the ANC, the organisation initiated a number of internal commissions to investigate (whether fully and impartially is still the subject of controversy) the abuses which several MK soldiers had suffered after the mutiny. The command structure of Mbokodo was also revised; Mzwai Piliso was redeployed; and a code of conduct was drawn up and implemented.

Unlike most of the guerrilla armies or rebel paramilitary forces of the late twentieth century, MK adopted a code of conduct and most cadres adhered to a strict discipline. Underlying the code was the idea that MK was a 'political army'. 'Our armed struggle is a continuation of our political struggle by means that include armed force,' declared the MK Military Code. This meant that, unlike many of the armed groups in Sierra Leone, Uganda and elsewhere, nobody was forced into MK. Children who wished to join (and there were many) were sent first for schooling until they were adults. The code prohibited assault, rape and cruelty;

71

bullying and intimidation; abuse of power, theft or forcible seizure of goods; the use of drugs; and even insulting or obscene language. This stringent code of behaviour and personal morality in the main prevented members of MK from descending into the kinds of acts that young men with automatic rifles and enormous power have used against civilian populations in other contexts. As the Military Code stated: 'Umkhonto is a people's army fighting a people's war. We fight to liberate our oppressed and exploited people. We fight for their interests. Umkhonto has no mercenaries, no paid soldiers or conscripted troops. It consists of the sons and daughters of the most oppressed, the most exploited sections of our people. For these reasons we claim with pride and truth: Umkhonto is the Spear of the Nation.'

While MK, like its 'parent' liberation movement, the ANC, was committed to nonracialism and nonsexism, the demographics of MK reflected the nature of apartheid society. Apartheid society was racist and sexist to the core, the most oppressed group being the African majority, which shared with the ruling white minority highly patriarchal values. The overwhelming mass of MK members were young black men. On the one hand, the profile of MK was not so different from armies all over the world: like them, it was drawn from young working-class men, the 'cannon fodder' of political and economic elites in warfare throughout human history. On the other hand, there were some distinctive features of MK: it consisted of a majority of Africans, who followed certain cultural practices and beliefs that marked them off from others. They were also, as an oppressed people, highly motivated to effect change and to improve the future not only for themselves, but for their parents and their own children.

Most armies struggle with gender issues and suffer from gender imbalances. MK was no different. Women had a hard time of it in MK. They were sometimes used and abused, despite the stated commitment to gender equality and the frequent quoting of Samora Machel's famous statement, 'The liberation of women is a fundamental necessity for the revolution, the guarantee of its continuity and the precondition for its victory.' Some of the experiences of women in MK have been sensitively documented by Raymond Suttner, who quotes Diphuo Mvelase: 'There was a situation where in our army there were very few women and they come into the army, officers will jump for them, all of them, and use or misuse their powers and the authority they have to get women. This led to some nasty situations. Comrade Chris [Hani] established this Rule 25 – it was a new rule – that no officer will have a relationship with a new recruit because it is an unfair relationship ... people complained about it. But it was observed.' Though rape was strictly prohibited and punished, the psychosexual stresses of thousands of young men living together in conditions of deprivation were considerable.

As for admission to MK, Motumi notes that 'training was unconventional, and there were no educational entrance requirements, as is normally the case with liberation armies. Prospective MK members only had to be against apartheid and have enough courage to take up arms. It was purely a volunteer army, with ill health or age the only grounds for exclusion.' Most of those who joined MK had little education and came from working-class backgrounds. Many comrades today who consider themselves to have been fashioned into disciplined revolutionaries by MK are not ashamed to speculate that they would have ended up as township gangsters or unemployed alcoholics if they had not 'joined the struggle'.

MK had the usual selection of late-twentieth-century weapons, many of Eastern European origin, used in the protracted guerrilla wars in Asia, Africa and South America. These included the AK47 semi-automatic assault rifle, the ubiquitous Kalashnikov referred to in township songs simply as the 'AK'; RPG7 grenade launchers or 'bazookas'; limpet mines; hand grenades of various descriptions; anti-tank mines and anti-personnel mines; and various other explosives, rifles and handguns. Yet most people who died in the liberation struggle from 1960 to 1994 were not victims of these weapons. A small number died in the bombing of buildings or were killed with AK47s. Many thousands – the overwhelming majority of those who died – were either shot by the South African Police or killed with the unsophisticated weapons of hand-to-hand combat in Africa – the *panga* (or machete), the *kierie* (knobbed stick) and the stone. And a horrifying number were killed by fire, burnt to death by means of the 'necklace' or on pyres of tyres or wood. While there are those like Anthea Jeffery who argue that the strategy of the ANC and MK was to engage civilians in a 'people's war' in which precisely this kind of killing was encouraged, this argument does not stand up to the evidence when it comes to the operations of MK.

One of the most interesting examples of restraint in the pursuit of guerrilla warfare is the case of MK's landmine campaign in 1985–7, which it subsequently put a stop to of its own accord. It should be noted that the landmine campaign took place before there was a widespread international lobby for the banning of anti-personnel mines. At the time landmines of various kinds were being widely used by all sides in the anti-colonial wars raging in Angola, Namibia and Mozambique. Indeed, South Africa is one of the few countries in the subcontinent involved in the liberation wars of the second half of the twentieth century not to have been left the devastating legacy of vast tracts of land infested with thousands of lethal mines.

At the ANC's conference in Kabwe in 1985, renewed emphasis was placed on MK operations in rural areas. Late in the year MK began to use anti-tank mines in rural areas on the border of South Africa. Between November 1985 and July 1987, MK units crossed from Zimbabwe and Swaziland into the northern and eastern Transvaal, an area of large commercial farms owned by white farmers. The units involved in this campaign planted a number of mines, resulting in 30 explosions, which caused 23 deaths. The prime targets of these landmines were military patrols of the police as well as the SADF. While the farming areas on the border were declared 'designated areas' by the government, the ANC considered them to be 'military zones' and the farmers 'security force personnel' and not civilians. The object of MK strategy was to reduce the SADF military presence in the area, thus creating 'space' for guerrillas to infiltrate across the borders and become based inside South Africa. MK members were under 'strict instructions to do careful reconnaissance in order to avoid civilian casualties' but this proved to be 'more difficult than anticipated', as the ANC indicated in its submission to the TRC in 1997.

In addition to reconnaissance to identify routes used by military vehicles, the selection of weaponry was of critical importance in the attempt to avoid civilian casualties. This lay behind the decision of MK's leadership to use only anti-tank mines, and not anti-personnel mines at all. As the ANC stated in its submission to the TRC, 'With regard to landmines, we feel it is critically important to point out that the ANC never used anti-personnel mines, specifically because we were concerned to avoid civilian casualties. The ANC used only anti-tank mines, which require at least 300 kg to detonate, because our primary targets were the military patrols on roads immediately next to borders. The mines were laid overnight so that they would be triggered when the SADF patrolled early the next morning. It was reasoned that because farmworkers generally did not have transport and moved around on foot, they were unlikely to be affected.' At the time, the ANC justified its use of landmines in the border area by reference to the Geneva Conventions.

On 16 December 1985, a landmine exploded under a vehicle on a farm in the Messina district. Two families of white farmers were game-watching from the vehicle when the mine was detonated. Four children, between three and nine years old, were killed as were two women; four other people were injured. Mr J.F. van Eck, one of the survivors, recalled at the TRC: 'Do you know how it feels to be blasted by a landmine? Do you know how it feels to be in a temperature of between 6000 and 8000 degrees? Do you know how it feels to experience a blast that is so intense that even the fillings of your teeth are torn out? … Do you know how it feels to look for survivors, only to find the dead and the maimed? Do you know how it feels to see crippled loved ones lying and burning? … Mr Chairman, do you know how it feels to try to cheer up a friend while your own wife and two children lie dead?'

Of course, given the indiscriminate nature of landmines, black civilians, adults and children, were killed and injured along with white. Despite the ANC's justification of the strategy on the grounds that white farmers had become *de facto* part of the security forces, and that the South African regime 'took steps towards obliterating the distinction between the civilian and military spheres', the death of children and farm labourers was not part of the plan. After a few such mines had been detonated by farmers' trucks or trailers, and a number of civilians had been killed, including black farm labourers and young children of white farmers, the ANC decided that the use of mines needed to be reviewed in terms of its principled decision not to cause civilian casualties. In late 1987 Oliver Tambo called all members of MK headquarters to a meeting and expressed his concern at the number of 'unnecessary civilian casualties'. 'MK HQ ordered that the laying of anti-tank mines should be halted.' This abandonment of the mine-laying strategy was one of the most remarkable illustrations of restraint shown by an armed opposition movement, especially in the context of the time in which not only anti-tank mines, but anti-personnel mines too, were widely accepted and used as weapons of war. Although MK did have anti-personnel mines in its armoury, access to such weapons was strictly controlled: units requesting anti-personnel mines had to satisfy the Revolutionary Council (the decision-making body on military strategy) that they would not be used except in specific cases of retreat from ambushes by enemy personnel. On occasion their use was authorised in this way, and they were used as well in Angola to protect MK camps, but there is no evidence that they were used in military operations inside South Africa. That as weapons they were inherently arbitrary in their destructive power and should thus be banned was not under debate at that stage.

The official position of the ANC that it was civilian casualties that resulted in the decision to halt the mine-laying campaign has been reiterated by MK's Military Intelligence head Ronnie Kasrils: 'This landmine campaign … was terminated when we realised the impossibility of avoiding civilian targets. We did so even knowing that our campaign was putting the regime under tremendous pressure.' On closer analysis, it seems that the pressure was less on the regime than on the ANC itself, as the use of landmines proved counterproductive in terms of strategic-military aims as well as in terms of propaganda. There was considerable publicity given to the civilian deaths due to mine explosions, and this may have had some influence on the ANC's decision to end the campaign. However, from testimony to the TRC and from interviews with ANC leaders it seems that the decision was based not so much on external pressure as on internal discussion within the MK and ANC leadership and on the evaluation of the effectiveness and costs of the mine-laying strategy. Most importantly, the operations were counter-productive: the campaign had a negative effect on MK logistical lines, and did not achieve its purpose of allowing arms to be brought deep inside South Africa and stored there, nor of allowing MK to establish bases inside the country.

The military and strategic failure of the landmine

campaign can also be illustrated by the fate of the MK units involved. After the initial blasts in December 1985 the ANC claimed responsibility and the South African security forces immediately set out to track down the perpetrators. Shootouts followed in which some of the cadres were killed, some captured, and others disappeared and were suspected to have been secretly killed and buried by the security forces. Only two members of these units were arrested and charged with murder; they later applied for amnesty from the TRC together with one member who had escaped either capture or death.

Those who stood trial were Mthetheleli Mncube and Mzondeleli Nondula. Mncube had been in the unit which laid the mines in December 1985. He was then redeployed a year later as part of a five-man unit which crossed into South Africa from Zimbabwe on 24 December 1986. Wearing blue-grey denim overalls, the cadres carried backpacks containing landmines and other weapons. On Christmas Day, a white farm owner came across the cadres and alerted the authorities. The security forces made contact with the group the following day and killed three of them. One escaped but was tracked down and killed the following day. The fifth member of the unit, Mncube, was captured. While the police were taking him to Messina on the back of a *bakkie* with the bodies of his dead comrades, he managed to seize a gun, kill the two police escorts and escape. On 7 January 1987 he was tracked down and recaptured.

After a trial in 1988 Mncube and Nondula were sentenced to death. In addition to the murder and attempted murder of those who died or were injured in the explosions, Mncube was charged with the killing of the two policemen. He and Nondula were convicted of murder, attempted murder, terrorism and contravention of the Arms and Ammunition Act. In 1992, in terms of the indemnity agreement between the ANC and the National Party government, they were released. In 2001 Nondula and Mncube were granted amnesty by the TRC for the landmine explosions, which had resulted in gross human rights violations.

What can be concluded about MK's use of landmines? At the time, the decision to end the landmine campaign in 1987 was primarily a strategic one based on a 'cost-benefit analysis'. However, the prior decision to use anti-tank rather than anti-personnel mines was taken essentially because of humanitarian concerns, based on the ANC's policy to avoid the loss of civilian life and its understanding of the indiscriminate nature of the use of such weaponry. As Ronnie Kasrils later remarked, 'We never contemplated using anti-personnel mines, as easy and convenient as these would have been, because we knew how indiscriminate they would be.'

5

# Reaping the whirlwind, 1984–9

The 1980s, the third decade of the armed struggle, opened up greater opportunities for MK and the ANC than ever before and, at the same time, greater challenges. The new decade began with exciting developments inside South Africa: the Release Mandela Campaign and the public distribution of the Freedom Charter for the first time since the 1950s. 1980 was declared by the ANC to be the 'Year of the Freedom Charter'. At the same time a whole new generation of students, youth, women and workers began organising around their own local demands and interests and gradually linked these to national political demands for a nonracial, nonsexist, united and democratic state.

From 1979, the ANC developed a growing influence on the emerging mass democratic movement inside South Africa. In some cases, such as the extraordinarily well-organised and influential Congress of South African Students (COSAS), the ANC gave direction to its formation through carefully placed underground cells. In other instances, the organic local resistance to apartheid generated new trade unions, youth organisations, residents' associations and NGOs, which could be influenced more subtly to support the ANC's broad position and become part of the 'Charterist' movement. From 1979 through to 1983, when the United Democratic Front was formed, the ANC strategy of mass mobilisation and building a mass base was highly successful. More and more, the black, green and gold ANC flag started to appear in public places, from funerals to cake sales in support of worker strikes.

In a statement released in June 1980 the ANC declared: 'Unite! Mobilise! Fight on! Between the anvil of united mass action and the hammer of the armed struggle we shall crush apartheid!' This powerful slogan, which was taken to heart, captured the spirit of the strategy outlined in the so-called Green Book, which the ANC had drawn up after some of its senior leaders visited Vietnam in the late 1970s and learnt about the conduct of a 'people's war' and the importance of building a base among the masses before trying to infiltrate guerrilla units. Grassroots mobilisation and organisation took place as never before, and united mass action became the order of the day in townships and on campuses around South Africa.

From September 1984, when the 'township uprisings' began, the opportunities for MK to prosecute a people's war opened up as never before. Some (though by no means all) urban townships were mobilised and organised to an unprecedented degree. By early 1986, the movement had in some areas effectively removed the official Black Local Authorities and taken control over their own communities. The ANC's call to 'render the country ungovernable, make apartheid unworkable' was being put into practice, by ordinary people, through their own actions and tactics.

This extraordinary achievement in the townships of Port Elizabeth was described by the senior security policeman H.B. du Plessis in his testimony to the TRC in 1997. He appeared before the Commission to apply for amnesty for the killings of the PEBCO Three, a trio of community leaders who were abducted and murdered by a covert unit of the Security Police in April 1985. One of the PEBCO leaders was Sipho Hashe, an MK veteran of the 1960s, who had been released in the early 1980s and built up the mass movement in Port Elizabeth.

According to Du Plessis, 'they started ... with the establishment of firstly the area and street committees. They exercised complete control over the masses. The instructions which they wanted to carry out or carry through to the masses were done via these channels. To give you an example, if there were any boycotts these people were told to carry it through and to ensure that they took place. As a matter of fact they were compelled to do so. PEBCO led the meetings where all these organisations were invited and had turns to speak and made their contributions, which were then conveyed to the community. They formed a unity to do what they wanted to do ... I can tell you quite honestly that Port Elizabeth was ungovernable and I want to go even further and say that PEBCO was in control here ... The councillors' houses were burnt down; I won't say all of them but many of them were attacked. They had to resign, they were forced to resign and this created a vacuum: that is, that the third tier of government collapsed. Petrol bomb attacks were made on the houses of policemen to such an extent that the policemen withdrew from the black areas, together with their families. There were school boycotts, schools were burnt down, vandalised. All buildings that had anything to do with the government [were] destroyed or burnt down. There were rent boycotts, bus boycotts. Streets were blockaded. At a stage in certain areas trenches were dug in which the Casspirs [armoured police vehicles] fell and then could not get out and petrol bombs were then thrown at the police. Soft cover vehicles were impossible to drive with and we had to do so in convoys. Delivery vehicles in the areas were burnt out. The consumer boycott was on and off.'

The problem was, where did this extraordinary uprising fit into the ANC's revolutionary strategy? At what point would these local manifestations of popular power translate into an onslaught on the apartheid state at national level?

While the ANC had extensive influence on the mass movement through its underground operatives, former Robben Island prisoners and supporters, there remained the difficulty of establishing consistent channels of communication with local command structures and infiltrating MK cadres. At its national conference at Kabwe, held at the height of the uprising in South Africa in mid-1985, the ANC formally adopted the strategy of people's war and envisaged the deployment of MK cadres into the country, acting in concert with the masses. All the same, the bitter fact is that most MK cadres continued to remain in the camps in Angola. So if not MK, who was prosecuting the ANC's strategy of people's war, of making the townships ungovernable and apartheid unworkable? Who was arming the masses in preparation for insurrection? The short answer is that the people were doing it themselves. Stealing small arms, creating homemade weapons, devising tactics of urban guerrilla warfare against riot police, they formed their own paramilitary units and prosecuted the strategy of the movement.

These youth formations in the urban townships were sometimes referred to simply as comrades, indicating their political allegiance to the liberation movement. But in some cases they formed themselves into *de facto* paramilitaries or militia called in the Eastern Cape *amabutho* (which means 'organisation' though traditionally it refers to a regiment or military formation under Shaka).

Here these 'MK wannabes' organised themselves according to MK military hierarchies and carried out MK strategy as they understood it.

Local *amabutho* were not formed on instructions from MK, though they developed working relationships with the MK cadres who were coming in and out of the country. The *amabutho* were structured into 'bases' each of which had its own area of operations. They spoke of 'engaging the enemy' in military terms. Though the *amabutho* took general direction from the political leadership, they made their own decisions about operational tactics. The *amabutho* also linked in with ANC underground networks that had been set up to arrange passage for those – many thousands – who wanted to go into exile and 'get training and guns' so as to come back to fight, better equipped. For the majority of those who left, this was effectively the end of their involvement in the struggle. Many stayed for years in exile, coming back during the transition period and never getting to put into practice their new-found military skills and equipment.

Those who stayed 'on the ground' fighting inside the townships saw themselves as the 'cutting edge' of the struggle. The *amabutho* relied primarily on their own handmade weapons: petrol bombs, primus stove bombs, and a crude dart-throwing pipe gun called a Skorpion. Another source of weaponry was the guns they obtained from attacks on security force members. Lastly, there were some weapons that reached the *amabutho* through underground MK networks, and on occasion they were accompanied by training. As one commander reported: 'MK guys were coming and saw that we needed training, so they taught us how to shoot, how to crawl, all that stuff. They did it in the night time, in Soweto [on Sea in Port Elizabeth], in any open field. They trained us in how to handle armoury, hand grenades and all that stuff.'

The *amabutho* did not have sophisticated strategies but employed creative military tactics, using whatever was available to them. While they did not express it in such terms, their major achievement was threefold: to create a 'liberated zone' in parts of certain townships, such as Soweto on Sea; to establish 'no-go zones' for the security forces; and to frustrate all attempts of the security forces to move freely around the townships, by digging 'Casspir traps' or trenches. Attacks on the trapped vehicles, luring soldiers outside, and then killing and disarming them, were also part of their offensive repertoire.

Ronnie Kasrils has described the situation where townships were made 'no-go areas' as one in which 'the rudimentary organs of people's power' were created. But it was not clear how this situation – characterised by the Marxist Workers' Tendency as 'pre-revolutionary' – was going to transform into a full-out revolutionary assault on the apartheid state. Martin Legassick, who consistently criticised the militarism of ANC leaders, argued that the claims of the ANC 'vastly exaggerated the situation and created completely unrealistic expectations among those that they reached'. Even at the time it was noted that the state 'retained its strong social basis in the white areas' and that the ANC, while successful in gaining mass support among the African majority, had not succeeded in creating 'significant splits in the ruling class' so as to undermine the state apparatus at its core. There were few white soldiers or policemen killed by the liberation movement, whether by MK or by *amabutho*.

Mtiwabo Ndube summarises the achievements of the Port Elizabeth *amabutho* in this way: 'the movement was getting inside the country and establishing a base. But the major work was done by internal forces, *amabutho* ... the ANC sent a group of guys to train *amabutho*, because we were learning from struggles in other countries, that normally in military struggles people must be armed, and I remember the first area that was taken over was Soweto [on Sea]. Guys were beginning to read books of Che Guevara; that we must dig trenches, the Hippos [military vehicles] would fall into the trenches – that was done in Soweto. People began to study the township, we would go up from New Brighton to Soweto via the sewer line – it was maybe five kilometres, the sewer line. Even today we can go there and move under the ground; the police would move around on top, and the guys would move arms underground. There was a lot of community involvement, people were supporting the struggle – all [house] yards in PE were open to the gaps so that you could move, you don't have to move in the street, you could move between houses, and all houses in PE had to [remove] their [street] numbers, so there was no numbering in the streets; this was one of the things we learned from Che Guevara; let's turn the township into a bush, let's be like fish in the water, all those things.'

In response to the township uprising the

apartheid regime imposed first a partial State of Emergency in 1985 and then a national State of Emergency, which lasted from mid-1986 until the end of 1989. For three and a half years, the security forces had extraordinary powers to detain without trial, to deploy military troops in urban residential areas, and to control people's movements through curfews and cordons. The use of these powers – in particular the detention of thousands of community leaders – effectively decapitated the uprising. By 1988 the regime was confident that it had regained control and could implement another round of elections to the Black Local Authorities, which had been destroyed by the uprising.

This period, which has in retrospect been characterised as a 'stalemate' in the sense that neither side could prevail in the conflict, saw MK's actions peak inside the country. There were 300 armed attacks in 1988 alone (as compared with 44 attacks in 1984). The period also saw the escalation of the informal war between the ANC (including the UDF and MK) and Inkatha in the KwaZulu homeland. Finally, it was during these years that the ANC took the decision at a high level to initiate and implement Operation Vula.

Operation Vula came about in response to the realisation that the weak link in the ANC's revolutionary strategy was the communication between the internal and external movements. More and more it seemed necessary and indeed paramount to strengthen the underground in South Africa. From 1987 Vula was put in place through the infiltration and recruitment of highly secret operatives as part of an underground structure. While respected for its members' discipline, and regarded as a crucial 'missing link' in the struggle, Vula exhibited two fundamental problems. The first was that by the time it became a functional network, it was too late; the moment of insurrection had passed, and the negotiations process was on track. The second was that even after the turn to negotiations Vula operatives were still concerned with preparations for a seizure of state power, bringing in and storing weapons, whether as a 'back-up strategy' or with the intention of effecting an armed uprising. Consequently, when the government got wind of Vula and made public its existence during the transition period, it was able to paint the ANC as negotiating in bad faith.

In the late 1980s, a decisive development within

the region with bearing on the fortunes of MK was the course of the Angolan war. Many hundreds of MK cadres engaged in battle in the 1980s in support of the Angolan army on the 'northern front' against Jonas Savimbi's UNITA forces and their allies, the SADF. Approximately a hundred MK soldiers died in these hostilities. The protracted battles at Cuito Cuanavale in 1987–8 proved costly for the SADF and served to bring South Africa to the negotiating table and the conflict to a close. This led to the implementation of UN Resolution 453 and ultimately to the independence of Namibia. But it also led to the closure of MK's Angolan camps and the removal of thousands of cadres to camps even further from the home front.

While those who were deployed on operations in South Africa were envied by their peers, they suffered an appallingly high rate of attrition: they were more often than not captured and jailed, or else killed in combat. Those who were arrested were usually subjected to torture; put on trial, they were invariably convicted and harshly sentenced. Other MK units ended up in deadly combat situations referred to as 'skirmishes' or 'shootouts' in ANC and police documentation. For many MK cadres, death was preferable to surrender or capture. Some of the stories of MK in the period 1987–9 illustrate the tragic heroism of these last operations before the suspension of armed struggle in August 1990.

Military experts like to talk about the 'rate of attrition', the rate of loss of personnel. MK suffered a very high rate of attrition, being faced with an enemy of huge military superiority. MK members put it more simply: they expected to be 'either captured and tortured, or killed', as one member explained. Despite the high probability of this outcome, they were keen to be deployed in the 'forward areas'. They were in fact more than keen: their commitment was absolute, and their preparedness to sacrifice themselves was at the level of the fanaticism of suicide bombers. But they were not suicide bombers: their tactics did not envisage killing themselves in order to kill as many civilians as possible. Instead, they anticipated heroic shootouts with their enemy, dying with honour, avoiding capture, and refusing to break under torture. And in some cases this was precisely what happened.

Nokuthula Simelane, one of the few women MK operatives deployed in South Africa, did not break under torture. Her bravery in the face of humiliation and agony was acknowledged even by her torturers, who are believed to have killed her and secretly disposed of her remains. Her story has been told in the film *Betrayal* (2006) by Mark Kaplan.

Welile Bottoman talks about the bravado with which young MK cadres in exile imagined they would handle their expected confrontations with the South African security forces. Some said they would fight to the death; others that they would commit suicide rather than surrender. Some vowed that they would never be caught. 'Like the "last bullet" and "never-never" comrades, I told myself, enemy soldiers should never catch me alive. Last bullet comrades were comrades who swore they would never be caught alive by the Pretoria regime. They swore they'd keep aside one bullet, which they would use for suicide should it be clear that they were about to be arrested or captured in their missions. "Never-never" comrades were the soldiers who would never be caught. How they would ensure that was unclear.'

This commitment to fight to the last is well illustrated by another story from the Eastern Cape. By early 1986, the informal settlements of Port Elizabeth bordering on the townships of Kwazakhele and Zwide were controlled by *amabutho*. These 'no-go zones' provided a limited space for MK to infiltrate and operate within. By mid-1986, when the national State of Emergency was declared, MK was keen to take advantage of the township uprising and the networks that had been established. Commanders who had entered South Africa in other areas were deployed to Port Elizabeth. If the strategy of people's war and popular insurrection through arming and training the masses was going to be effective anywhere, then it would be in the townships of Port Elizabeth. The Security Police had already declared them ungovernable and 'no-go zones' for ordinary policemen after white conscripted soldiers in the SADF had been lured from their armoured vehicles and killed by *amabutho*.

In this situation, the Security Police set up a special 'terrorist tracking unit' to deal with MK members who were deployed to carry out this strategy. By mid-1987, the MK units in Port Elizabeth had been infiltrated and all their members were wiped out in a shocking series of killings. Their associates in the underground network were detained, tortured and put on trial. The death of the final member of the unit is reminiscent of the heroic tales of legendary outlaws like the Kelly Gang in Australia, vividly described in Peter Carey's *True History of the Kelly Gang* (2000), and portrayed in the movie *Ned Kelly* (2003). In the case of the MK unit led by Sonwabo Mdekazi, a similar story emerges.

MK Commander Mdekazi, known by his nom de guerre as Thanduxolo ('lover of peace'), was deployed to Port Elizabeth with his unit, consisting of himself, the political commissar Pinki Mpindi (MK Thabo Moloi) and Ntsikelelo Mketi (MK Zola). They had already been involved in a skirmish with the Ciskei homeland police at a roadblock on the way, and Mpindi had a bullet wound in his head. When they arrived in Port Elizabeth, local township activists including Vuyo Kwinana, Mzolisi Dyasi and 'Shuta' Mkongi arranged safe houses, food and shelter for them, and agreed to recruit committed young activists for military training by the MK comrades.

Unaware that the car had been traced, the unit went to the safe houses arranged for them. Mketi hid in Dyasi's girlfriend's shack in the informal settlement of Veeplaas. Mketi had been around earlier in the decade, assisting the *amabutho* with weapons during the 1985 uprising. Mdekazi found a 'safe house' with the assistance of an old prison comrade, and Mpindi went to stay in a shack in Motherwell with his cousin, Nombini Zini (Booi).

About two weeks later, on 7 July 1987, Mpindi and his cousin Nombini were killed in a 'skirmish' with police in Motherwell. At 6.15 am, police surrounded the shack. They claimed to have come under fire, and ordered the occupants to step outside. They then used a Casspir armoured vehicle as a 'breaching device' to crush the shack; afterwards two bodies were found in the ruins. It is not clear whether Mpindi and his cousin were killed by police gunshots or by the vehicle. Some comrades believe that Mpindi shot himself to avoid being captured alive.

Two days later, on 9 July, police in Kwazakhele were fired upon with automatic weapons. Mketi and comrades from the area who had been provided with arms engaged the police in an attempt to avenge their comrade's death. 'We burnt tyres because we wanted the police in Casspirs to come and extinguish those tyres. But unfortunately those guys in green uniforms came to put out those fires. We attacked them with AKs and hand grenades … Mketi was leading that, and we attacked them there.

We had grenades, and AKs ... Fortunately no one died there in that skirmish.' One policeman was injured, and a massive search followed.

The next MK cadre to be tracked down was Mdekazi. At 4.30 am on 5 August, police surrounded the house in New Brighton where he was sleeping. He was shot dead where he lay. The third member of the unit was Mketi. He was assisted by the underground activist Thozama Phoebe Mani, the girlfriend of Mzolisi Dyasi, as well as by Dyasi's cousin, Lungu Sokupha. Mketi, it seems, was betrayed by one of his township comrades, and was ambushed by Security Police while walking in the township streets at night. Despite sustaining five bullet wounds and a broken arm, he managed to escape, and was treated in secret by a sympathetic township doctor, Dr Maqina.

By this stage, the police were tracking the unit down systematically, and it was inevitable that they would catch up with him. Mketi's comrades advised him to go back into exile, but he refused. Ten days later, the security forces found the shack in the informal settlement of Veeplaas where he was hiding. At 3.30 am on 10 December 1987, the shack was surrounded. Mketi and Mani were shot and killed, and the shack was bulldozed by armoured vehicles. According to a police report, two people were 'fatally injured in a skirmish'. The police claimed that there was 'heavy resistance from cadres' and that automatic weapons were used against them. They had retaliated by using an armoured vehicle as a 'breaching device' to drive over the shack.

Dyasi later vividly described what he understood as a 'shoot to the death'. 'So in Veeplaas there was this skirmish; they fought, they fought, they fought, for many minutes, many minutes. And again, I know this guy shot himself. Okay, let me tell you. This guy would never surrender, never. And I suspect he was the first man to shoot. He saw the torches of the police approaching. My aunt was still alive, she was right there inside the house. This was my aunt's house. And my girlfriend was there. And my cousin was there, Sokupha. Apparently they saw torches, so they knew there were police outside, surrounding them. And Mketi started to shoot. But the police never tried to effect any arrest. They never even used loudhailers to say "Come out, we are the police, surrender" as they used to do. But they never did that. No.

'Apparently they stopped the cars 100 metres away or so, then they went to the house with their rifles and their torches on top. So I presume that this guy saw them first, or whoever saw them first, and then there was a shootout because I knew Mketi would never surrender. He didn't want to leave, because he said his commander died here, and his political commissar died here. Pinki [Mpindi] was the political commissar. He said they both died here, and I am going to die here.'

The circumstances of these 'skirmishes', as they were termed by the police and the guerrillas, were to become an interesting point under international humanitarian law. In all three cases, police surrounded the houses in which the suspects were sheltering. In two of the three episodes, they used armoured vehicles to destroy the dwellings, but before doing so they fired into the houses, killing the occupants. They alleged that on all three occasions the 'terrorists' were armed and fired back at them. Who shot first is a moot point: in the case of Mdekazi, the police claimed with pride that they had shot first. In normal circumstances the police would be obliged to inform the suspect that he was under arrest and to give him a chance to surrender. But in these instances, the police insisted they were in a 'war situation' and, anticipating enemy fire, did not wait for the enemy to shoot first.

On the other hand, we should note that the MK guerrillas adopted the attitude that they would never surrender and, if cornered, would rather die fighting. It seems that in all three episodes, the MK operatives were aware of their impending deaths and were prepared to fight to the bitter end – the 'never-never' comrades described by Bottoman. It is possible that one or even two of them were 'last bullet' comrades who took their own lives. All in all, six people, MK soldiers and members of their underground support networks, died in this series of skirmishes in Port Elizabeth in 1987.

'Fight to the last bullet' was not an order, but a decision and action indicative of absolute commitment. In 1988, one of the few rural battles (and possibly the last) between MK and South African security forces took place. This battle, which occurred on 28 March 1988 on an island in the Mutale River in the nominally independent homeland of Venda, is described here by one of the participants, Patrick Bobelo, as an illustration of a 'conventional' confrontation between MK and the SADF. The teller of the story, who is now a Colonel in the SANDF, was interviewed for the SADET project in 2002. A COSAS activist from Queenstown in the Eastern Cape, he had been recruited into the ANC underground as a student before leaving for Angola in the early 1980s. In Angola, he received specialised training, being sent to Cuba, and was made platoon commander, then commissar, and finally a unit commander. He was first engaged in battle on the front against UNITA in Angola, before being deployed to the 'forward area' of Zimbabwe, from where the unit crossed into South Africa:

'Then the Commander came to Zimbabwe, [Joe] Modise, and briefed us on what we were going to do, gave us operating material. Then he left and we got into the boats and crossed the Limpopo back into South Africa, from Zimbabwe ... We didn't go during the day, it was getting dark when we started, we had big packs on our backs, we were armed ... As we were moving, first thing in the morning, in the bushes, we heard some movement of trucks, the SADF. We were ... going to operate around Venda, we were going to a base in the Kruger National Park ... On the third day, the 28 March 1988, as we were crossing a certain river ... the rear patrol, the person right at the back, gave an indication that we were being followed. So I said okay, let us take defensive positions, and I went to look. It was the SADF. We were in a safe position, camouflaged …. As they were approaching … I gave instructions to fire. They were eight metres away, in the water. We utilised hand grenades, we killed the first group that were in the water. The person about to get in was carrying something … and we were shooting at him. We didn't shoot him dead, he managed to crawl and made some communication.

'I said to them, Well, let us say goodbye because we might not know what will transpire in this battle. The only feeling you have, either you are going to die, there is nothing else to feel. We were told when we were trained that the best thing is for you to fight to the death rather than be captured, because we might not be able to take the torture methods that were being used, and we might compromise. That was the problem. So it's either allow yourself to be captured, or you fought, which was the best thing. When you shake hands with your comrades you have known for three years … you hug. All of you shake hands. That's what we did. We were going to fight to the last of our bullets. As long as we are alive. There is nothing else to do. We are not going to surrender. We have to make sure that each bullet is counted.

Otherwise we will be wasting bullets to shoot people at a distance, instead of a clear target. So people went back to our positions, there was heavy fire from the ground forces, from the side of SADF.

'The fighting started at five to six in the morning, it went right on to past eleven, one o'clock. Then one of the guys got shot in the head … Then as we were fighting, the machine gun … managed to hit one of the helicopters … As he shot, it crashed not very far from us, it exploded … As time goes, one of our guys was shot, as well as the machine gunner. They were killed. Three were killed. The other one was shot in the thigh. I said we must change position, it seems as if they can spot us. So what happened … it didn't function, so I gave instructions as we were moving from that place that we must destroy it. Then we left to find another position. They destroyed it with grenades. The injured guy we took with us … We managed to crawl to the other side, we fought, at round about half past six they withdrew. That was nice, perhaps they felt this was a big base, but we were not yet a base. So the guy who was shot couldn't move, that was a problem. Fortunately not far there was a village. Though he said we must kill him, we did not kill him. If you can't take someone, you can ask to be killed. You have to choose the best option. It is not wise to kill someone. He can do that himself. So we took him to a village in Venda, and asked those people to keep him, we would come back and fetch him. So the three of us, the four of us left. The other guy was left to keep watch over this comrade. They killed him the following day, but he managed to take nine out of the SADF. Not the one we left, the one who was keeping watch. He had a clash with them, managed to kill nine of them.

'We were now in the KNP [Kruger National Park], the second day as we were in the park … the KNP has everything, lions, tigers; it was not easy. In the bush, you have to take that risk. If you have the heart to do it, it is your choice. KNP was chosen because it has the animals etc, it was safer, we would be watching all the time ourselves, and with armaments we could hide in the bush, and it was better fighting terrain. So we managed to go back to Zimbabwe. Then … they took us back to Harare, our people came and fetched us, and we were reunited with the units. I was called to Lusaka, to be debriefed by Cde Chris Hani and Steve Tshwete (commissar) about what happened.'

Five MK members were killed and one injured

in this battle: those who died were Daniel Nkabinde (MK Vusi Mthembu), Mlungisi Velaphi (MK Mzimkulu Goduka), Sipho Nkosi (MK Peter Molotsi), Oupa Lukhele (MK Dan Mabaso) and Abram Moroe (MK Happy Batho). Despite Bobelo's claims, only one security force member is recorded as having been killed in the battle, a Venda Defence Force soldier called Robert Tshiambaro.

6

# The end of armed struggle

Underlying the desperate accounts of the battles, skirmishes and bombings, urban and rural, which we have described, is a great irony: that while MK cadres were being exhorted to 'escalate the armed struggle' in preparation for a revolutionary seizure of power, their political leaders were entering into covert negotiations with the enemy. This was later to be justified publicly as a 'two-track' strategy: maintaining the pressure of armed struggle while exploring the preconditions for negotiations. But there is a strong argument that the wisdom of Oliver Tambo and Nelson Mandela lay in their understanding that a negotiated settlement was not only possible but the right thing to do. Far from being a 'miracle', it was the outcome of a realistic assessment of the political context: the collapse of the Soviet Union, the withdrawal of South African forces from Angola, the independence of Namibia, the pressure on the government from South African businessmen to keep the economy running, and the mounting cost in human life of the continually escalating armed struggle.

As we have seen, the situation on the ground in South Africa had reached stalemate in the late 1980s. By 1988 the security forces had regained control over the urban townships, stabilising them through brute force, unrelenting State of Emergency regulations and the removal of township leaders. They had also prevented 'ungovernability' from expanding into areas outside the African townships, and had protected their white support base, in the main, from being affected by the violent resistance. While the apartheid regime could maintain control through force, it could not gain legitimacy; and while the ANC had gained legitimacy, it could not win state power. It was in this context that a negotiated settlement became an attractive option to both sides. Moreover, the changing international context made a negotiated settlement not only desirable but unavoidable.

1989 saw the revival of the Mass Democratic Movement (MDM) and a period of *abertura* (opening) or liberalisation, in which the regime allowed some popular mobilisation as it prepared for negotiations. The release of the Rivonia trialists and of State of Emergency detainees, and a range of interesting local-level negotiations that involved recognising the leadership of the mass movement, all indicated that something momentous was imminent. P.W. Botha's replacement by F.W. de Klerk as head of the National Party and then State President constituted the formal leadership change which allowed the 'doves' within the NP to pursue their strategy of a negotiated settlement.

Notwithstanding the signs that change was on the cards, the unbanning of the ANC on 2 February 1990 and the subsequent release of Nelson Mandela came as a shock to all but those in the inner circles of the 'negotiation faction' in both the ANC and the NP. A movement that had been illegal for three decades was now legal. The last of those imprisoned on Robben Island were set free and the exiled leaders of the ANC were allowed to return home. These developments were a source of great joy to most South Africans. And yet there was widespread confusion about the way forward. What made things even more difficult was the escalation of violence in

KwaZulu-Natal and in the townships of Gauteng, where the struggle seemed far from over.

It should be obvious that the decision to suspend the armed struggle in August 1990 was incomprehensible to many MK cadres. Having vested everything in the armed struggle, and believing that the people's war strategy would be successful, they found it hard to accept that their leaders were insisting on a negotiated settlement. Resource documents on the purpose and content of negotiations were distributed to ANC members to ensure that activists both in MK and in the mass movement understood what the shift in strategy entailed. Even so – and especially in the areas of most violent conflict, such as the Natal Midlands – the desire to rely on MK and keep fighting to the bitter end was strong. As Wonga Bottoman has written, 'The last years of the eighties decade, even though we had earlier heard of talks, even understood the concept thereof, were confusing to us as soldiers, used to Victory or Death slogans.'

The ANC suspended its armed struggle in terms of the Pretoria Minute of August 1990. The suspension was an act of extraordinary restraint, and posed a great challenge for the MK leadership, who had to enforce it. Here were thousands of armed and trained young men, coming back into South Africa prepared for revolution, having been waiting in frustration in camps in Angola and elsewhere for years. Not only was there no triumphal welcome for the heroes from exile but there was still a deadly struggle going on in parts of the country. It seemed obvious to these MK cadres that they should respond to the demands of their constituency, the urban and rural people who supported the ANC, by supplying them with guns and assisting them to defend themselves against the enemy. To the rank-and-file it seemed that the MK leadership lacked a clear policy or strategic approach. As Mark Shaw has said, 'Cadres … regarded the leadership, with notable exceptions, as inept and inefficient: this antagonism was displayed at the first national MK conference held in Venda in 1991.'

Throughout the transition period, the ANC kept up its 'two-track' strategy: of negotiating but maintaining a military capacity for the purpose of self-defence and as a back-up in case the negotiations broke down. MK was in the invidious position of being formally on ceasefire but constantly receiving pleas for assistance and for guns. Consequently the ANC helped to set up, arm and train so-called Self-Defence Units in response to the initial wave of attacks on urban communities in late 1990. The rationale for the SDUs was set out by the ANC in a pamphlet entitled 'For the Sake of our Lives':

1.5 Self-defence structures need, by definition, to be para-military. They differ from all the other forms of organisation referred to, including street committees.

They must be tightly structured to repulse aggression and ensure law and order, they need a specific command and control system; their members must be trained and have a high degree of discipline.

1.6 At present, in the light of the Groote Schuur and Pretoria Minutes, Umkhonto weSizwe (MK) alone cannot undertake the task of our people's defence, although this is a right we need to forcefully demand and struggle for.

The August 6 cease-fire does not neutralise MK. It has an important role to play. MK cadres, particularly ex-prisoners and those due to return from exile, must play a leading and active role in the establishment of the defence.

1.7 As we proceed to establish defence units so we must raise the demand for the right of self-protection.

The ANC argued later before the TRC that as it had ceased military operations under the terms of the Pretoria Minute of August 1990, any acts perpetrated by the SDUs were not under its control; rather, they were under the control of the local communities in which they were based. The ANC's submission to the TRC noted that 'We do not have records of MK's role in SDUs since they were not HQ-controlled structures'. At the same time, the ANC submission stated: 'Senior ANC leaders decided that selected SDUs should be assisted in those areas of the Reef which were hardest hit by destabilisation. Selected members of MK, including senior officials from the command structures, were drawn into an ad-hoc structure to assist with the arming of units and to train and coordinate efforts in self-defence in these communities; this was done on a need-to-know basis. At MK's conference in Venda in August 1991, the President called on MK to fulfil its responsibilities in defending communities under attack.'

The transitional violence was devastating and, despite the best of intentions, MK was an integral part of it. Far more dangerous than a disciplined guerrilla army is a dispersed network of armed and poorly trained youth under no centralised command. Returning MK soldiers went back to their communities of poor and unemployed people, only to be confronted by thousands of frustrated youths demanding action, wanting to prove themselves against the enemy, waiting for a decisive victory. Some of the worst incidents of violence in this period involved internal power struggles that got out of hand. Local power politics, a strong element of territoriality and the desire for local control all played a part, and were interwoven with a discourse of community defence and reaction against criminal or 'anti-social' elements.

One of the more tragic incidents was that of the Moleleki massacre in the township of Katlehong. In this case, 13 persons later applied to the TRC for amnesty for the killing of nine victims on 7 December 1993. All people who died in this incident, and even the perpetrators, were members or supporters of the ANC. The killers were members of the local SDU; those murdered, members of the ANC Youth League; all were young men residing in the same community. The youths were taken forcibly into the open bush and systematically killed, one by one, by residents of their own community. One of the perpetrators explained his actions to the TRC amnesty committee as follows: 'The SDU was to defend the community and they were harassing the community, that was the reason. An order is an order. It was difficult even on my side to kill them. I did not have any option, I was just ordered and I know that their families are bereaved but there was nothing I could do really.'

As we can see, this applicant used the military language of hierarchy and orders to justify his actions. Yet the amnesty committee of the TRC did not consider the decision made in his SDU as having the status of an order of a constituted military formation. Such a case highlights the problem of holding people to account for acts of paramilitary sectarian violence. While the youths involved in committing these acts were not trained soldiers, neither were they simply members of an unorganised mob. Perceived threats to the integrity of the community in which they lived, and the level of poverty and deprivation experienced there, often combined with experiences of brutalisation by the security forces, gave them the personal motivation to undertake these acts. But their motivation was always situated within a broader political framework, which labelled those identified for attack as 'enemies of the liberation struggle'.

Most MK cadres returned from exile in 1991–2, after the suspension of armed struggle. Many of those who had waited in camps in Tanzania and elsewhere were desperate to get home, suffering from shortages of food and basic supplies. When they finally did arrive home, they had literally nothing and came back to little more. Instead of returning as heroes, able to meet the expectations of their loved ones, they became a burden on their already struggling families. And while the logistics of their return were handled reasonably well, the joy at finally going back home was tempered in many cases by confusion and disorientation. By the end of 1992, some MK returnees were protesting at the ANC headquarters because of their dissatisfaction with the way they were being treated.

In 1993 Jacklyn Cock conducted interviews with returned MK soldiers for the Military Research

Group. By that stage, 17,000 exiles had returned, of whom approximately 5,000 were MK cadres. Overwhelmingly young men, they recounted having suffered extreme hardships in exile; many experienced post-traumatic stress and various kinds of trauma, manifested in insomnia and disorientation upon returning to 'normal life'. Most of them came back to situations of poverty and overcrowding. A great number were ill, with HIV/AIDS, malaria, diabetes or hypertension. Many dealt with their stress by abusing alcohol. A minority became 'bandits', using their access to weapons to engage in violent crime.

During 1991–3, MK members who had returned continued to be threatened by the South African security forces. At the same time, MK continued to recruit and train new members, operating from the nominally independent Transkei homeland after General Bantu Holomisa took power there in a military coup in 1987. From the late 1980s through to 1994, the Transkei was a base for MK. While the ANC denied that MK had engaged in any military operations after the suspension of armed struggle, it maintained its right to recruit and train soldiers. This formed part of the 'back-up' plan in case the negotiations process collapsed completely. As with the IRA and the Good Friday Accord, the suspension of armed actions meant a ceasefire but not the disbandment and demobilisation of armed forces. This left a dangerous situation where militant and angry youth were still seeking to join MK and obtain access to weapons, while the National Peace Accord was trying desperately to ensure that the appropriate climate for negotiations prevailed.

As Jacklyn Cock wrote, 'There was a lot of romance in MK. MK people went out [of South Africa] with dreams. They thought they'd come back in camouflage uniform, marching through the streets of Pretoria with their heads held high. But there was no romance in exile – just demoralisation.' And when they returned, there was no 'new world' awaiting them: just the same poverty they had left behind. Publicly, much noise was made about the contribution MK cadres could make to reconstruction in South Africa – they were young, energetic, relatively well-educated, disciplined and motivated. Suggestions included using MK cadres in a mass literacy programme, as had been done in Nicaragua and Mozambique. And yet most did not have their skills channelled in a positive direction.

Many wished to continue to be soldiers, not knowing any other life. As one of Cock's informants told her, 'I am a soldier. I want to be a professional soldier proudly defending my country. I have spent many lonely years moving from country to country, crossing rivers and eating anything from grass to snakes, trying to liberate South Africa. Nobody has sat down to listen to my pain and suffering in exile. I have done all this to liberate my country. I am a soldier.'

MK began to prepare for the integration of these cadres into a new South African army by 'professionalising' them, sending them on training courses in Western and African countries such as Zimbabwe or in India. But some were not enthusiastic about the prospect of spending their lives as soldiers: 'I am not interested in being a professional soldier. War is lousy. We were forced into it. The army is a wasteful, non-productive institution … I despise war.' And many more self-destructed either mentally or physically. 'All my time is free. I think and think and think. I just feel like shooting everybody. I am not even allowed to do gardening at home. It could help my frustration. That is why I drink too much. One day they will wake up and find me dead.'

Nor did the deaths of two prominent leaders help to alleviate the grim situation. On 10 April 1993 Chris Hani, the popular and charismatic Chief of Staff of MK from 1985 to 1992, was assassinated outside his home by white right-wing fanatics. Shortly thereafter, on 23 April, the day of Hani's funeral, the president of the ANC, Oliver Tambo, died. The death of these two leaders in the penultimate year of the transition left MK cadres without their champion (Hani) and their symbolic father (O.R.).

During the difficult and violent transition process, negotiations about the future of MK and its enemy, the SADF, began. Mark Shaw notes that the talks were delayed until March 1993 – nearly three years after the unbanning of the ANC in February 1990 – because the SADF was understood by the apartheid government to be a 'bulwark' or a 'stable core' during the transition. In terms of the negotiations process, the SADF and the homeland armies were declared 'statutory forces' while the armies of the liberation forces were designated as 'non-statutory forces'. This category included MK, by far the largest of the non-statutory forces, as well as the Azanian People's Liberation Army (APLA) and the Azanian National Liberation Army (AZANLA).

The Transitional Executive Council agreed upon in the negotiations process established a sub-council on defence. This set up a Joint Military Co-ordinating Council, chaired jointly by MK and the SADF. Finally, a plan was produced for integrating all the former armies into a new South African National Defence Force (SANDF). The process of demobilisation and integration began after the first democratic elections of April 1994. It was at midnight on 26 April that the SANDF came into existence. A Certified Personnel Register was set up, and MK headquarters was tasked with drawing up a register of all MK members. These cadres were called to designated assembly points and screened for inclusion into the new SANDF. This process was arduous and problematic, and many MK members were turned away. From late 1994 and through 1995 more protests by MK members took place.

By May 1995, some 15,000 of the 34,000 non-statutory forces members (comprising 28,000 MK and 6,000 APLA soldiers) had reported to assembly points. While they are referred to by some analysts as guerrillas, it should be noted that many thousands had not been formally trained nor engaged in guerrilla operations; they included some of those informally trained inside South Africa, including SDU members, but (somewhat unfairly) not the *amabutho*. Mark Shaw estimates that up to 40 per cent chose not to report to assembly areas, and instead were 'informally demobilised' or 'self-demobilised'.

By June 1995, nearly 12,000 members of the non-statutory forces members had been integrated into the SANDF. It was expected that in the end around 14,000 MK members would be integrated into the SANDF. If Motumi's estimate that there were no more than 10,000 to 12,000 MK members who received formal training outside South Africa is accurate, then most of this number were absorbed into the new army.

The main problems faced by MK cadres during and after the transition were – and still are, in many cases – social integration, poverty and unemployment. Many of those committed to being professional soldiers were incorporated into the SANDF. Some joined the SANDF for lack of any alternatives; others did not get to be incorporated, even though they had no alternatives.

As with all cases of change, there was a sense of

loss and sadness when MK was absorbed into the SANDF. Beloved symbols and practices could no longer be retained; and 'Hamba Kahle Mkhonto' was no longer sung at the gravesides of deceased soldiers.

More generally, many former MK cadres feel that the SANDF did not accept or accommodate their positive values and practices: their political understanding, commitment to justice and dedication. Some military experts like the late Rocky Williams have regretted that several of MK's unique qualities were not adequately recognised and embraced, including its creativity and ingenuity. The idea of civilian defence, he argued, was something that could have been more effectively adopted. MK did bring much that was positive to the SANDF: for one thing, the legitimisation of the defence force, in a political context in which an army not accepted by the majority of people could potentially pose a serious threat to stability and democracy in the country and the region.

Many MK members who died in Angola of malaria or in combat with UNITA or were killed in the townships are no longer publicly remembered. This kind of history always raises controversial issues around who is remembered and how: who was a hero, who a perpetrator, who a martyr and who a victim? The MK members who laid landmines were awarded the status of heroes, but their victims disputed this. Thozama Mani, who was killed by the police in an attack on an MK base, was recorded by the TRC as a victim of human rights violations by the police; but her comrades who were MK members are not considered victims, as they 'died in combat'. Many of those who died in combat or in other ways are not remembered at all. Yet were the victims of malaria in Angola any less deserving of being remembered and honoured than those who died in prison?

The way in which people involved in the struggle are remembered or forgotten in South Africa today seems quite arbitrary. There are memorials to some MK heroes and martyrs: Solomon Mahlangu in Gauteng; Coline Williams and Robbie Waterwitch in Cape Town; Vuyisile Mini and his comrades in Port Elizabeth; Nokuthula Simelane in KwaZulu-Natal. Many of the stories of hundreds of other MK cadres who died in combat or disappeared at the hands of the Security Police have not yet been properly documented. There is not even a comprehensive list of those who died. The National Prosecuting Authority is engaged in a continuing process of finding out what happened to those who disappeared and, where possible, locating and exhuming their remains and restoring them to their families and communities.

A Wall of Remembrance has been erected at Freedom Park in Tshwane. Here the names of all those who died in South African conflicts are recorded. This is, however, a controversial process, very much still in progress.

# 7

# A sober assessment of MK

There is a strong case to be made that MK's armed struggle will be remembered as an example of a just war conducted with considerable restraint. The argument is all the more compelling if the South African liberation struggle is compared with other civil wars in Africa – in Sudan, for instance, or the DRC – in the second half of the twentieth century. Even if the ANC's armed struggle is set alongside that of its subregional allies, FRELIMO in Mozambique, SWAPO in Namibia and the MPLA in Angola, we can see that its modus operandi was different; the costs of the war to the local population were far lower; and the psychological as well as physical and infrastructural effects were less far-reaching. Just one manifestation of this is the absence of anti-personnel mines littering the countryside, as they do in Southern Sudan, Angola and Mozambique, preventing rural people from obtaining a livelihood from the land. South Africa, already 50 per cent urbanised and dependent for food on large-scale commercial farming rather than subsistence farming, did not suffer the same economic and social disruption that other African countries experienced as a result of civil wars or liberation struggles.

The nature of the ANC and MK as organisations was of crucial importance to the kind of war that was waged and the costs of that war. The argument is straightforward: the ANC was – and still is – a political organisation and MK always fell under its discipline and political direction. Unlike the IRA or the Sudan People's Liberation Army, MK was controlled by a 'parent body' with a sophisticated and relatively democratic collective political leadership. Certainly, there were many weaknesses and failures in the ANC's leadership and decision-making structures. Nevertheless, it maintained its coherence and unity for the three decades of the armed struggle, and consistently gave direction to and imposed restraints on the strategies and military doctrines of MK. Though the ANC leadership did not interfere with MK on a day-to-day operational and logistical basis, it did intervene in such matters as the Military Code, the use of landmines, the mutinies in Angola, and major changes in strategy. As Makhanda Senzangakhona and his colleagues write in *Mkhonto weSizwe: Within Living Memories*: 'The ANC and the military wing, MK, fully appreciated that armed struggle was a political struggle by means which included the use of military force. The basic tenet was that the primacy of political leadership must remain unchallenged and supreme, and that all revolutionary formations, armed or not, were subordinate to that leadership. The understanding was equally that the struggle had to be won through all-round political mobilisation that was to accompany military activities. In the envisaged people's war, MK was perceived as the core of the people's army and constituted the cutting edge of political efforts.'

The figure of deaths due to political violence in South Africa between 1960 and 1994 is commonly given as between 20,000 and 30,000. Of these MK was responsible for only a small fraction. The truly disturbing statistic as far as deaths are concerned comes from the period of the transition to democracy, i.e. February 1990 to April 1994, when 14,000 to 15,000 deaths occurred. For most of this period, MK had suspended its armed struggle. The total number of deaths from political violence in South Africa is probably close to 21,000 and includes some 5,500 who died in the 1984–9 township uprisings and another 700 or so in the 1976–7 students' uprising. The figure does not include South Africans who died in other countries. Even if the statistics are an undercount, and the number who died was closer to 25,000 or even 30,000 in the period between 1960 and 1994, the fact remains that more people died in the four-year transition period, after MK had suspended its armed struggle, than in the preceding three decades.

On both its own tally and that of the apartheid security forces, MK was directly responsible for the deaths of some 250 people in the period from 1960 to mid-1990. According to the former South African Police spokesman Herman Stadler, testifying before the Truth and Reconciliation Commission, between 1976 (when MK operations resumed inside South Africa) and 1990 (when the ANC suspended armed struggle) MK killed 240 people and injured 1,694. Of the 240 deaths, 24 civilians were killed by landmines. The ANC's own figures, listed in its submission to the TRC, are remarkably close to Stadler's: MK caused the deaths of 107 civilians and 131 security personnel in the period from 1960 to 1990.

MK was an army of over 10,000 trained soldiers, most of whom were never deployed in South Africa, with access to more weapons than they could use. That in three decades of armed struggle MK killed only 240 people is an extraordinary outcome, resulting from a combination of ineffectiveness and restraint. The costs of MK's war were definitely lower than they could have been if we consider the killing fields in other arenas of conflict in Africa at the same time. In fact, the costs were highest to MK itself – to its own dedicated cadres who laid down their lives, suffered torture, or spent years or decades in prison or in appalling conditions in training camps in Angola, and to their families.

If the South African liberation struggle is compared with other twentieth-century wars, the death toll, whether measured in absolute terms or as a percentage of the population, is remarkably low. On Matthew White's website 'Historical Atlas of the Twentieth Century', the entry for 'Death tolls for multicides of the twentieth century' lists the South African struggle under the heading of 'minor atrocities' (in which the numbers of dead are in the thousands but less than 21,500). The Zimbabwean liberation war falls into the next category of 'lesser multicides' (between 21,000 and 60,000 dead); the Mozambican and Angolan wars of independence until 1975 and the civil war in Sierra Leone belong to 'mid-range wars' (58,000 to 120,000 deaths); while the Angolan civil war until 2002 belongs to the category 'secondary wars and atrocities' (between 120,000 and 620,000 deaths). 'Major wars and atrocities' (over 620, 000 deaths) include those in Sudan, Ethiopia, Rwanda and Mozambique until 2002.

But can it really be argued that the relatively low cost in terms of human lives was due to the moral judgement of MK's leadership? While it certainly played a part, there were other factors that made MK's armed struggle less destructive than many others. The key was the very nature of the state that MK was trying to overthrow. The apartheid state was a strong, stable, authoritarian state. Like similar regimes in Argentina or Chile at the time, it relied on a combination of powerful security forces, legitimacy among an elite of the population, support from Western powers, economic stability, and a semblance of law and order. As in former totalitarian regimes in communist countries, levels of social control were high, and policing was tight. It was in former African colonies where the state's power had dissipated that the most brutal violence occurred: after Mobutu's reign ended in the DRC, or after the Portuguese departed from Mozambique and Angola, leaving the liberation movement governments to fight wars against the 'proxy forces' of the West. Unlike Batista's Cuba or Somoza's Nicaragua, the apartheid regime was not a fragile and corrupt state, and its considerable military might was maintained throughout the Cold War, both with and without Western support.

The ANC-aligned historian Bernard Magubane argues that the 'alleged failure' of the armed struggle was not due to the 'adventurism' of MK, but rather to the overwhelming brutality of the apartheid state. Yet this argument is also tenuous, if the apartheid state is compared with other authoritarian regimes of that era, such as the military regimes of Chile and Argentina, which caused thousands of civilian opponents to disappear. The number of people 'disappeared' by the apartheid security forces can be counted in the hundreds, if that. Torture and abuse, in violation of the Geneva Conventions of war, were applied mercilessly against MK, it is true. Indeed, both sides made claims to morality and legitimacy but both violated the Geneva Conventions. It would have been more surprising if they had abided by them.

It is incorrect to characterise the apartheid state as a military regime of unrestrained brutality. Although immensely powerful in military and police terms, it was neither a military dictatorship nor a totalitarian police state. Even at the height of resistance to apartheid, when a State of Emergency and various security laws were used to contain dissension and revolt, there was still a degree of relative social and economic normality in South Africa. Infrastructure continued to function; transport was available for the public; businesses sold goods; municipal water and sewerage systems continued to function. None of this is to suggest that the apartheid state was in any way 'better' than its successor or that the decision to take up arms against such an oppressive system was in any way unjustifiable. Rather, it is to recognise that one of the reasons why the struggle against apartheid did not develop into the absolutely devastating war that it could have been was the very nature and power of that state.

In all the three decades of armed struggle there really was little hope of MK being successful in either the military sense or the classic revolutionary sense. There could be no seizure of state power, no insurrection, no defection of the security forces to the side of the revolution, no liberated zones in the countryside where peasants could begin to build the new society. The limited experiments in 'people's power' in the townships in the 1980s did not challenge the power of the central state. On its part, the state did not use a small fraction of its military capacity to deal with MK. Even so, MK suffered a high rate of attrition among its members, their operational lives inside South Africa were typically short, and the costs to those who survived and to their families and networks were extremely high. In military terms MK has to be judged one of the least effective armies in modern history.

And yet, at the ideological level, it was another matter entirely. As far as legitimacy and popular support are concerned, MK had won the war against the apartheid regime by 1986. As Howard Barrell paradoxically remarks, 'the more the armed struggle failed, the more it succeeded'. In the end the ANC and its military wing, MK, achieved their objective of a national democracy in South Africa. Though MK did not defeat its enemy on the battlefield or seize power by force, yet if it is seen as an army acting with restraint under military discipline and with due observance of the international conventions of warfare, which averted a possibly devastating civil war, and at the same time contributed to raising the morale of an oppressed people and delegitimising an oppressive regime, then it cannot be judged a failure.

Yet neither can MK be regarded as responsible for the overthrow of apartheid. The 'struggle' was conducted by millions of ordinary South Africans, without weapons or military training, who joined trade unions, refused to carry passes, boycotted their local councillors, refused to vote in apartheid elections and, in a myriad of other ways, undermined the apartheid system and made it unworkable. It was not military operations that caused apartheid to implode. At the same time the defiance and revolt of ordinary South Africans were part of a broader strategy that the liberation movement adopted, and were seen as complementary to the armed struggle.

In conclusion, MK soldiers were undoubtedly South African patriots, fighting a just cause, to end the apartheid regime and create a united and inclusive national democratic state. They achieved this objective, whatever criticisms can be made of the strategies they used or the nature of South African society today.

143

# Sources and further reading

There is a growing body of writing on MK, both accounts of the personal experiences of cadres and commentary by academic historians and political and military analysts. The list given here is by no means exhaustive

### Autobiography and biography
Thula Bopela and Daluxolo Luthuli, *Umkhonto we Siswe: Fighting for a Divided People.* Alberton: Galago, 1999

Wonga W. Bottoman: *The Making of an MK Cadre.* Pretoria: LiNc Publishers, 2010

Connie Braam, *Operation Vula.* Johannesburg: Jacana, 2004

Luli Callinicos: *Oliver Tambo: Beyond the Engeli Mountains.* Cape Town: David Philip, 2004

Scott Couper, *Albert Luthuli: Bound by Faith.*

Pietermaritzburg: UKZN Press, 2010

Mark Gevisser, *Thabo Mbeki: The Dream Deferred*. Johannesburg: Jonathan Ball, 2007

Jeremy Gordin, *Zuma: A Biography*. Johannesburg: Jonathan Ball, 2008

Ronnie Kasrils, *Armed and Dangerous: My Undercover Struggle against Apartheid*. Oxford: Heinemann, 1993

Ronnie Kasrils, *The Unlikely Secret Agent*. Johannesburg: Jacana, 2010

Gerard Ludi, *Operaton Q-018*. Cape Town: Nasionale Boekhandel, 1969

Raymond Mhlaba, *Raymond Mhlaba's Personal Memoirs: Reminiscing from Rwanda and Uganda*. Pretoria: HSRC Press, 2001

Bruno Mtolo, *Umkonto we Sizwe: The Road to the Left*. Durban: Drakensberg Press, 1966

James Ngculu, *The Honour to Serve: Recollections of an Umkhonto Soldier*. Cape Town: David Philip, 2009

Padraig O'Malley, *Shades of Difference: Mac Maharaj and the Struggle for South Africa*. New York: Viking, 2007

Rashid Seedat and Razia Saleh (eds.), *Men of Dynamite: Pen Portraits of MK Pioneers*.

Johannesburg: Ahmed Kathrada Foundation, 2010

Joe Slovo, *Slovo: The Unfinished Autobiography*. Johannesburg: Ravan, 1995

Janet Smith and Beauregard Tromp, *Hani: A Life Too Short*. Cape Town: Jonathan Ball, 2009

Harold Strachan, *Make a Skyf, Man!* Johannesburg: Jacana, 2004

Raymond Suttner, *Inside Apartheid's Prisons: Notes and Letters of Struggle*. Pietermaritzburg: University of Natal Press, 2001

Mzeli Twala and Ed Benard, *Inside MK: Mwezi Twala – A Soldier's Story*. Jonathan Ball, 1994


**Political, military and human rights analysis**
Howard Barrell, *MK: The ANC's Armed Struggle*. Johannesburg: Penguin, 1990

Howard Barrell, 'Conscripts to their age: African National Congress operational strategy, 1976–1986', DPhil thesis, Oxford University, 1993

Gavin Cawthra, Gerald Kraak and Gerald O'Sullivan (eds.), *War and Resistance: Southern African Reports*. London: Macmillan, 1994

Janet Cherry, 'Just war and just means: Was the TRC wrong about the ANC?' *Transformation*, 42, 2000

Janet Cherry, 'Armed struggle and sectarian violence: South Africa and Northern Ireland compared' in Alf Ludtke and Bernd Weisbrod (eds.), *No Man's Land of Violence: Extreme Wars in the 20th Century*. Gottingen: Wallstein Verlag, 2006

Jakkie Cilliers and Markus Reichardt (eds.), *About Turn: The Transformation of the South African Military and Intelligence*. Halfway House: Institute for Defence Policy, 1995

Jacklyn Cock, 'The forgotten people: The need for a soldiers' charter'. IDASA Occasional Papers no 47, 1994

Max Coleman, *Crime against Humanity: Analysing the Repression of the Apartheid State*. Cape Town: David Philip, 1998

Adrian Guelke, 'Interpretations of political violence during South Africa's transition'. *Politikon*, 7, 2, 2000

International Council on Human Rights Policy: *Ends and Means: Human Rights Approaches to Armed Groups*. Geneva: The Council, 2000

Anthea Jeffery, *The Truth about the Truth Commission*. Johannesburg: South African Institute of Race Relations, 1999

Anthea Jeffery, *Peoples War: New Light on the*

*Struggle for South Africa.* Johannesburg: Jonathan Ball, 2009

John Kane-Berman, *Political Violence in South Africa.* Johannesburg: South African Institute of Race Relations, 1993

Martin Legassick, 'Armed struggle and democracy: The case of South Africa'. Nordic African Institute, Discussion Paper 20, 2002

Tom Lodge, *Black Politics in South Africa since 1945.* Johannesburg: Ravan, 1983

Bernard Magubane, *South Africa from Soweto to Uitenhage: The Political Economy of the South African Revolution.* Lawrenceville, NJ: Africa World Press, 1989

Govan Mbeki, *Sunset at Midday.* Johannesburg: Nolwazi, 1996

Dale McKinley, *The ANC and the Liberation Struggle: A Critical Political Biography.* London: Pluto, 1997

Tsepe Motumi, 'The Spear of the Nation: The recent history of Umkhonto we Sizwe (MK)' in Jakkie Cilliers and Markus Reichardt (eds.), *About Turn: The Transformation of the South African Military and Intelligence.* Halfway House: Institute for Defence Policy, 1995

Tsepe Motumi, 'Umkhonto we Sizwe: structure, training and force levels (1984–1994)'. *African Defence Review*, 18, 1994

Laurie Nathan, *The Changing of the Guard: Armed Forces and Defence Policy in a Democratic South Africa*. HSRC Press, 1995

Padraig O'Malley, 'The Heart of Hope'. <www.nelsonmandela.org/omalley>

Jeremy Seekings, *The UDF: A History of the United Democratic Front in South Africa, 1983–1991*. Cape Town: David Philip, 2000

Mark Shaw, 'Negotiating defence for a new South Africa' in Jakkie Cilliers and Markus Reichardt (eds.), *About Turn: The Transformation of the South African Military and Intelligence*. Halfway House, Institute for Defence Policy, 1995

Vladimir Shubin, *ANC: A View from Moscow*. Johannesburg: Jacana, 2008

Paul Trewhela, *Inside Quatro: Uncovering the Exile History of the ANC and Swapo*. Johannesburg: Jacana, 2009

Rocky Williams, *South African Guerrilla Armies: The Impact of Guerrilla Armies on the Creation of South Africa's Armed Forces*. Institute for Security Studies Monograph Series no. 127, 2006

## Historical accounts

Janet Cherry, 'Hidden histories of the Eastern Cape underground' in SADET, *The Road to Democracy in South Africa*, Volume 4 (1980–1990). Pretoria: Unisa Press, 2010

Janet Cherry and Pat Gibbs, 'The liberation struggle in the Eastern Cape' in SADET, *The Road to Democracy in South Africa*, Volume 2 (1970–1980). Pretoria: Unisa Press, 2006

Stephen Ellis and Sepho Sechaba, *Comrades against Apartheid: The ANC and the South African Communist Party in Exile.* London: James Currey, 1992

Peter Harris, *In a Different Time: The Inside Story of the Delmas Four.* Cape Town: Umuzi, 2008

Bernard Magubane, Philip Bonner, Jabulani Sithole, Peter Delius, Janet Cherry, Pat Gibbs and Thozama April, 'The turn to armed struggle' in SADET, *The Road to Democracy in South Africa*, Volume 1 (1960–1970). Cape Town: Zebra Press, 2004

Rendani Ralinala, Jabulani Sithole, Gregory Houston and Bernard Magubane, 'The Wankie and Sipolilo campaigns' in SADET, *The Road to Democracy in South Africa*, Volume 1 (1960–1970).

Cape Town: Zebra Press, 2004

Makhanda Senzangakhona, Edwin Mabitse, Uriel Abrahamse and George Molebatsi, 'Mkhonto we Sizwe: Within Living Memories: Part One'. *Umrabulo*, 13, fourth quarter, 2001

Raymond Suttner, *The ANC Underground in South Africa to 1976*. Johannesburg: Jacana, 2008

Ben Turok, *The ANC and the Turn to Armed Struggle, 1950–1970*. Johannesburg: Jacana, 2010

### Official documents and testimony

African National Congress, *Statement to the Truth and Reconciliation Commission*, August 1996

African National Congress, *Further Submissions and Responses by the African National Congress to Questions Raised by the Commission for Truth and Reconciliation*. 12 May 1997

Truth and Reconciliation Commission of South Africa, *Reports*, Volumes 1–5. Cape Town: The Commission; Volumes 6–7.

# Index

Printed in the USA
CPSIA information can be obtained
at www.ICGtesting.com
LVHW060827090823
754308LV00002B/4

9 780821 420263